DATE DUE

NO 06 '91			
NO 20 '91			
MY 04 '92			
DEC 1 8 2013			

Katherine Anne Porter

Revised Edition

Twayne's United States Authors Series

Kenneth E. Eble, Editor

University of Utah

TUSAS 90

KATHERINE ANNE PORTER
(1890–1980)
Photograph by George Platt Lynes,
courtesy of Bernard Perlin.

Katherine Anne Porter

Revised Edition

By Willene Hendrick
and George Hendrick

Twayne Publishers
A Division of G. K. Hall & Co. • Boston

Katherine Anne Porter
Revised Edition
Willene Hendrick and George Hendrick

Copyright 1988 by G.K. Hall & Co.
Published by Twayne Publishers
A Division of G.K. Hall & Co.
70 Lincoln Street
Boston, Massachusetts 02111

Copyediting supervised by Lewis DeSimone
Book production by Gabrielle B. McDonald
Book design by Barbara Anderson

Typeset in 11 pt. Garamond
by Modern Graphics, Inc., Weymouth, Massachusetts

Printed on permanent/durable acid-free paper
and bound in the United States of America

Library of Congress Cataloging-in-Publication Data

Hendrick, Willene, 1928–
 Katherine Anne Porter.

 (Twayne's United States authors series ; TUSAS 90)
 Rev. ed. of: Katherine Anne Porter / George Hendrick.
 Bibliography: p.
 Includes index.
 1. Porter, Katherine Anne, 1890–1980—Criticism
and interpretation.   I. Hendrick, George.   II. Title.
III. Series.
PS3531.0752Z683   1988   813'.52   87–21246
ISBN 0–8057–7513–7 (alk. paper)

Contents

About the Authors

Willene Lowery Hendrick, a nurse, has published articles on nursing in professional journals and for many years has assisted her husband, George Hendrick, in his scholarly research and writing. They were recently coeditors of *On the Illinois Frontier: Dr. Hiram Rutherford, 1840–1848,* and they are at work on additional writing projects.

George Hendrick, professor of English at the University of Illinois at Urbana-Champaign, has published articles on Thoreau, Emerson, Whitman, Washington Irving, and Tennessee Williams. His books include *Henry Salt: Humanitarian Reformer and Man of Letters, Remembrances of Concord and the Thoreaus, Toward the Making of Thoreau's Modern Reputation* (with Fritz Oehlschlaeger), *Ever the Winds of Chance* (with Margaret Sandburg), and *The Selected Letters of Mark Van Doren.*

Preface

Katherine Anne Porter has a special place in American literature. The actual volume of the artistic work she chose to publish is relatively small but of extremely high quality. She received early critical acclaim for the short stories collected in *Flowering Judas*, and she added to her reputation with the publication of *Pale Horse, Pale Rider*, which contains three excellent short novels. After decades of work, she finally completed *Ship of Fools*, her first and only long novel, an immediate best-seller in 1962.

Porter was a highly personal writer, and this study begins with a biographical essay. Her life is of great interest to anyone studying her art, but until recently the facts about her background were scanty and largely incorrect. During her early years as a writer, she originated many fanciful stories about herself, a practice she continued over the years, culminating in the interviews she gave to Enrique Hank Lopez in the last years of her life, and which he published after her death as *Conversations with Katherine Anne Porter: Refugee from Indian Creek* (1981). Joan Givner's authoritative *Katherine Anne Porter: A Life* (1982) finally separated truth from fiction about much of Porter's life, and we are greatly indebted to that excellent biography.

In the chapters containing individual discussions of Porter's stories, we pay special attention to the settings, themes, and literary indebtednesses. We have grouped these stories under three headings. In "My Familiar Country" we show that Porter's artistic use of the Mexican scene changed over the decades, from seeing Mexican culture from the inside in "María Concepción" to the later stories of alienation. In the following chapter, entitled "The Native Land of My Heart," we discuss the stories of fictionalized autobiography that have the grandmother and Miranda as central characters. We have reordered the stories to emphasize the influence of the grandmother and southern society upon Miranda. In "To Tell a Straight Story," the last of the chapters on the short fiction, we discuss the stories with southwestern, universalized, Irish, and German settings, attempting at all times to show Porter's mastery of the short story and short novel form.

Porter's novel *Ship of Fools* received mixed critical notices, and we have included a section of reviews and criticism from America, England, and Germany. With the publication of Givner's biography of Porter and the often unreliable but revealing taped interviews with Lopez about her German experiences, we understand much more about the characters and political events of this novel. We have attempted to show the novel's complexity as influenced by Sebastian Brant, James Joyce, and Henry James.

In the chapter on Porter's nonfiction we pay particular attention to her collected reviews and essays, to the published sections of her never-completed study of Cotton Mather, to her long-delayed book on Sacco and Vanzetti, and to her *Outline of Mexican Popular Arts and Crafts*.

Porter was a conscious literary artist in the tradition of James and Joyce. Her stories show her great mastery of technique as she explores the human personality and society. She reordered, through art, the disorder of life. She was correct in her self-estimate: she was an artist.

To reduce the number of notes, we have appended in the notes for each story a list of the criticism we have found most pertinent. We have not given page numbers to quotations from Porter's writings, except for *Ship of Fools*, for the stories and the criticism are short and the quotations are easily found.

We are indebted to staff members of the British Library; the Brownwood, Texas, Public Library; the Fort Worth, Texas, Public Library; the Humanities Research Center at the University of Texas at Austin Library; the Frankfurt University Library; and the University of Illinois at Urbana-Champaign Library for their assistance, and to the publishing firm of Rowalt for its clippings on Porter. We are also deeply indebted to those who have previously written on Porter, for they have increased our understanding of her and her art, and we are especially grateful to Joan Givner, who read the manuscript and made many helpful suggestions.

Willene Hendrick
George Hendrick

Urbana, Illinois

Chronology

1890   Callie Russell (name later changed to Katherine Anne) Porter born 15 May in Indian Creek, Texas, daughter of Harrison Boone Porter and Mary Alice Jones Porter.

1892   Death of Mary Alice Jones Porter. Harrison Porter then moves with his four surviving children to Kyle, Texas, where the children are cared for by his mother, Catherine Anne (Aunt Cat) Skaggs Porter.

1901   Death of Catherine Anne Skaggs Porter.

1901–1905   Porters move to San Antonio where Callie attends the Thomas School for one year; moves to Victoria where she and her sister teach the arts; meets John Henry Koontz.

1906–1914   Marries John Henry Koontz; converts to Catholicism after her marriage; leaves her husband after seven years; works as a movie extra in Chicago in 1914; returns to Texas.

1915–1916   Divorced in 1915, takes the name Katherine Porter; becomes ill with tuberculosis in the fall of 1915; enters a charity hospital, then in 1916 a sanatorium near San Angelo, Texas; finally transfers to a hospital in Dallas.

1917   Employed as writer on the *Critic,* a Fort Worth weekly newspaper.

1918–1919   Reporter on *Rocky Mountain News* in Denver; dangerously ill with influenza.

1919–1920   Moves to New York where she works for a motion picture magazine, writes stories for children, prepares the story for a Mexican ballet.

1920   Travels to Mexico.

1921–1922   Returns to Fort Worth, then New York, where she writes her first mature story, "María Concepción."

1922–1929 Returns to Mexico to help prepare an exhibit of folk art; returns to New York; marries Ernest Stock in 1926 (later divorced); takes part in protests against the executions of Sacco and Vanzetti.

1930 *Flowering Judas;* returns to Mexico; receives a Guggenheim fellowship; Hart Crane her house guest.

1931–1932 Sails from Mexico for Europe; lives in Berlin; travels in Europe.

1933 Marries Eugene Pressly (divorced 1938); lives in Paris; *Katherine Anne Porter's French Song Book.*

1934 Enlarged edition of *Flowering Judas;* Harrison of Paris publishes limited edition of *Hacienda.*

1938 Marries Albert Erskine, Jr. (divorced 1942).

1939 *Pale Horse, Pale Rider.*

1942 Translation of Lizárdi's *Itching Parrot.*

1943 Elected member of National Institute of Letters.

1944 *The Leaning Tower and Other Stories.*

1952 *The Days Before.*

1962 *Ship of Fools.*

1965 *Collected Stories of Katherine Anne Porter.*

1966 Receives Pulitzer Prize and National Book Award for *Collected Stories.*

1970 *The Collected Essays and Occasional Writings of Katherine Anne Porter.*

1977 *The Never-Ending Wrong.*

1980 Dies 18 September in Silver Springs, Maryland; cremated and ashes buried at Indian Creek, Texas.

Chapter One
The Fiery Furnace and After

Katherine Anne Porter often spoke of the relationship between her past and her art. In her journal of 1936 she wrote that the "exercise of memory" is "the chief occupation of my mind, and all my experience seems to be simply memory, with continuity, marginal notes, constant revision and comparison of one thing with another. Now and again thousands of memories converge, harmonize, arrange themselves around a central idea in a coherent form, and I write a story."[1]

A knowledge of Porter's biography is, therefore, of value to anyone interested in her art, but the biographical information she revealed was often romanticized or patently false. Now that Joan Givner's *Katherine Anne Porter: A Life* has appeared, we can reconstruct much of Porter's past without the myths she carefully cultivated early in her career and continued charmingly to perpetrate until the end of her life. Any student of Porter's life and work is cautioned to view with discretion virtually everything she says about herself in interviews and in Enrique Hank Lopez's *Conversations with Katherine Anne Porter*.

Porter wrote in "Reflections on Willa Cather" that she had little interest in biography after the tenth year, for what is to be is determined by then: "The rest is merely confirmation, extension, development. Childhood is the fiery furnace in which we are melted down to essentials and that essential shaped for good." She understood the importance of truth in biography, but she could rarely admit the harsh truths of her own life, except in her fiction.

The Family

For years Porter claimed that Daniel Boone was one of her ancestors; then she decided that Daniel's brother Jonathan was one of her great-great-grandfathers. Both stories were fanciful. Though she was not descended from the pioneering Boones, she was born in a log cabin. Callie Russell Porter (she was named for one of her mother's childhood friends and later renamed herself Katherine Anne) was born in 1890 (not 1894, two years after the death of her mother, as she claimed for many years) in Indian Creek, Texas, the fourth child of Harrison and Mary Alice Jones Porter. Indian Creek was then a frontier community, and Callie was born in a two-room cabin. Though well educated for their time, her parents were poor. The Porters were members of the Methodist church, and Harrison Porter was Sunday school superintendent. Their life in Indian Creek came to an end in 1892 when Mary Alice Porter died not long after the birth of her fifth child, Mary Alice. The cause of her death was either tuberculosis or bronchitis—the stories vary—but clearly the hardships of frontier life and constant childbearing had weakened her health. The Porter children were, in order of birth, Annie Gay, called Gay; Harry Ray, whose name was changed to Harrison Paul and who was called Paul; Johnnie, who died in infancy; Callie Russell; and Mary Alice, named for her mother and called "Baby" by the family. The maternal grandmother, Caroline Jones, did not take the children into her home; she was grief-stricken after the death of her daughter and later died in an asylum.

Harrison Porter and his four children left Indian Creek for Kyle in Hays County, Texas, between Austin and San Marcos, to live with his widowed mother, Catherine Anne Skaggs Porter, known as Aunt Cat. She had been born into a slave-owning family in Kentucky, and although the Skaggses were not aristocratic planters, they certainly were a family of some means. Catherine Anne married Asbury Porter in 1849, and the young couple sold his Kentucky property for a thousand dollars and moved to Hays County, Texas, where they purchased 368 acres of land and owned a few slaves. The Civil War began not many years after the Porters moved to Texas, and hard times soon came to the family, as it did to virtually all southern families.

When Harrison Porter and his children moved into his mother's four-room home in Kyle, most of the family property was gone and the Porters lived in poverty. (There were no faithful old ex-slaves in residence, contrary to Porter's recollection in interviews and in her fiction, though one former slave, Aunt Jane, lived in San Marcos and would sometimes visit.) Aunt Cat was a hardy person: she bore eleven children, nine of whom she raised. Her husband and her male children apparently were either weak in character or poor and inefficient managers, while she was strong, resilient, and an excellent organizer and manager. She was also a stern Presbyterian (Porter in interviews made her into a rather charming tippler, which is undoubtedly fiction, though Aunt Cat very likely did not object to using liquor for medicinal purposes), and she had no hesitation in using corporal punishment to tame her high-spirited grandchildren. The most spirited and untamable was Callie, who characterized herself: "I was precocious, nervous, rebellious, unteachable, and made life very uncomfortable for myself and I suppose for those around me."[2] She, like her grandmother, was intransigent.

Although Katherine Anne Porter was to give out romanticized stories about those early years in Kyle—rooms filled with books, faithful ex-slaves in attendance, education in a convent school—the reality was quite different. The family of six was cramped together in a tiny house, and Harrison Porter, devastated by his wife's death, made no attempt to provide the economic necessities for his children. More affluent neighbors gave cast-off clothes to the Porter children. Callie, even then proud and defiant, felt the shame of poverty.

Aunt Cat was puritanical and a stern taskmaster, but she provided the only stability in the family. She was a storyteller of great ability, and from her Callie learned many of the arts of storytelling. Aunt Cat was also willful and domineering; her granddaughter later became as opinionated and domineering as she. Family life was again broken in 1901 when her grandmother died, but the essential Katherine Anne Porter had already been formed. She wanted to be a writer, and she said in one interview that at the age of six she wrote "A Nobbel—The Hermit of Halifax Cave."[3] She also had a burning desire to be an actress, and she acted in and directed plays in the yard of the family home. She was a consummate actress all her life.

With the death of the grandmother, the family began to break up. The house in Kyle was sold for ten dollars, and Harrison Porter borrowed two hundred dollars and moved to San Antonio, where Callie and Gay were enrolled as day students in the Thomas School, a private institution with Methodist leanings. Porter had only one year there and was not a good student, but she was exposed to classic books, music, art, and theatre. The school gave a temporary stability to her life, but her father, she wrote later, did not make a "reasonable effort" to pull the family "out of the hole they were in and let them go to rags and almost to death."[4] In addition, once his religious mother was dead, he turned against religion, and his agnosticism must have been unsettling to the adolescent Callie.

First Marriage

After the year in San Antonio, Harrison Porter moved to Victoria, and Callie and Gay opened a "studio of music, physical culture and dramatic reading." While she lived in Victoria, Porter met John Henry Koontz, a railroad clerk in Louisiana, and a member of a prosperous south Texas family of Swiss descent. The Porters soon moved to Lufkin in east Texas, and in 1906 sixteen-year-old Callie married Koontz. The ceremony was performed by a Methodist minister, but Koontz was Catholic and in 1910 Callie converted to Catholicism.

The marriage lasted nine years, but it was not a happy union and Porter lived with Koontz for only seven of those years. According to Joan Givner, because they were "drawn together for the most unsubstantial of reasons—physical attraction and, on Porter's side, a desperate need for financial and emotional stability—[they] found themselves swiftly disappointed and pushed each other into outrageous acts."[5] Porter may well have angered Koontz by her attentions to other men—all her adult life she was coquettish—and he may have abused her physically. Givner speculates that Porter was unable "to find any pleasure in sex" and that she discovered she could not bear children. "It seems likely, then," Givner notes, "that her first marriage reinforced her feelings of sexual confusion."[6]

Early Career

At the age of twenty-three, Porter took her first steps toward a career. She bolted from her unsatisfactory, barren marriage, and early in 1914 she went to Chicago, where she worked as a movie extra. Later, she was to tell several versions of this period of her life, but it seems clear that she was unable to establish herself in the acting profession and she returned South a failure. For the next few months, she looked after her sister Gay, then living in Louisiana where Gay's husband had abandoned his wife and children. Porter had another try at performing; she appeared on the lyceum stage, singing ballads and wearing a costume she made herself. Gay's husband returned, and much to Porter's disgust, Gay allowed him to remain. Porter, however, was determined to end her own marriage, and she soon divorced John Koontz, charging him with physical cruelty. She requested in her divorce petition that she be given the name Katherine Porter and that name change was made.

Her health had broken in Chicago, possibly from overwork and lack of food, and once again in Texas her health deteriorated. She was diagnosed in 1915 as having tuberculosis, and since she had no money, was forced to enter a charity hospital in Dallas. Her brother Paul, in the navy, was the only member of the family financially able to help her escape the horrors of that institution, and in 1916 she moved to Carlsbad, a well-run sanatorium not far from San Angelo. A fellow patient there, Kitty Barry Crawford, was a college graduate, a journalist, and with her husband owned a Fort Worth newspaper. When Porter recovered from her illness, after a stay in a Dallas hospital she moved to Fort Worth, where she was hired as a reporter on the Crawfords' paper, the *Critic*.

Preparing to Be a Writer

As a student at the Thomas School, Porter had access to classic works of literature; she was especially taken with Shakespeare's sonnets. In her early attempts at writing she imitated Laurence Sterne and in her reading she discovered Willa Cather, Henry James, W. B. Yeats, Joseph Conrad, and Gertrude Stein. By accident, she came across Joyce's *Dubliners,* which she read not with shock but as a revelation, "a further unfolding of the deep world of the imagination."[7]

At the *Critic* she wrote drama criticism and society gossip. She led an active social life in Fort Worth, but she soon followed Kitty Crawford, who was in Colorado because the mountain air was considered good for Kitty's weak lungs. There Porter became a reporter on the *Rocky Mountain News* in Denver; she worked at that newspaper for only a short time before she became a victim of the influenza epidemic of 1918 and almost died, an experience she later turned into one of her most compelling stories, "Pale Horse, Pale Rider." After her brush with death, she returned to the newspaper, where she reviewed movies, dramas, and vaudeville, wrote musical criticism, and published several interviews. She was a competent journalist, and her exposure to good and bad drama helped form her aesthetic theories.[8] She was ambitious and by the end of 1919 was ready to leave Denver for New York.

Life in New York and Mexico

In Greenwich Village Porter supported herself by doing publicity work for a motion picture company, writing stories for children, and ghosting *My Chinese Marriage* by M. T. F. (1921). She came to know several Mexican artists and worked with Adolpho Best-Maugard on a Mexican ballet for Pavlova. She wrote the story, and Best-Maugard painted the scenery. She was learning a great deal about Mexican art and culture and was soon offered a job in Mexico working on a promotional magazine. She remarked that her Mexican artist friends kept talking about the renaissance in Mexico and told her to go there instead of to Europe because, they said, "That's where the exciting things are going to happen." When she arrived in Mexico in 1920, that country was still in the upheaval of the Obregón revolution.

In this first phase of her life in Mexico, she was optimistic about the new government and about social and political revolutions. She wrote for the magazine, taught dance in a high school for girls, and met many of the leading artists, intellectuals, and revolutionaries of the country. She also moved among the jaded European expatriates in Mexico. She fell in love with Joseph Hieronim Retinger, but the affair ended badly. Her short stay in Mexico was, though, a time of great intellectual and artistic development, and her first mature fiction was built on her Mexican experiences.

While she was in Mexico, an American anthropologist named William Niven took her to his dig, where she heard the anecdote she later transformed into "María Concepción," one of her best short stories. Porter also saw and talked to the Indian woman around whom she fashioned the story.

Another of her famous stories came about as the result of her friendship with Mary Doherty, a midwesterner in Mexico helping women organize unions. Doherty, prim and puritanical, was visited by a fat revolutionary, and Porter, happening to see him singing to Mary, fashioned around this incident a story, "Flowering Judas," one of the masterpieces of modern short fiction.[9]

Mexico was in political turmoil, and Porter was accused of being a Bolshevik. Afraid of being deported or arrested, she left Mexico in 1921 and returned to Fort Worth where she began work on a paper published by Kitty Crawford's husband. Restless, she soon moved back to New York where she wrote articles about Mexico for the *Century* magazine. Her first major story, "María Concepción," was published in that journal in December of 1922. Before the story appeared she returned to Mexico, this time to help organize an exhibit of Mexican art and to write the exhibition catalog. With that catalog she began to formulate a coherent aesthetic view. As Givner has shown, Porter found that Mexican art derived its strength from its native roots, and she began to realize that she, as an artist, could draw on her native land and its people in her own fiction. The United States government did not recognize the Obregón government and would not allow the exhibit, which it called "propaganda," to tour this country. Frustrated, Porter returned to the United States. During the next few years, she worked at fiction, largely set in Mexico, had a series of lovers, and restlessly moved from the Village, to country retreats in New England, and back to the Village again.

Again she married, and again unwisely, this time to Ernest Stock, a twenty-five-year-old Englishman, an interior decorator and sometime painter, more than a decade younger than she. The year was 1926. For a time they lived in an artists' community in Connecticut, and from this unhappy marriage came her story "Rope." She soon bolted this marriage, but not before Stock may have transmitted gonorrhea to her. The infection produced such severe complications that it was necessary for her to have a hysterectomy. A pattern was beginning to develop in her love life, as Joan Givner notes: Porter was repeatedly finding herself attracted to men younger than she, men who resembled the handsome but weak father she remembered from her early childhood. [10]

During the middle and late 1920s she did extensive book reviewing for the *New York Herald Tribune,* the *New Republic,* and the *Nation.* In 1927 she joined the protests against the execution of Sacco and Vanzetti, and she went to Boston to demonstrate. She was arrested and bailed out several times, and was present outside the prison when the two anarchists were executed. Porter made many notes about her small part in the effort to save their lives, but she was not able to finish her account for five decades, when it was published as *The Never-Ending Wrong.*

Her short stories appeared infrequently, but in 1930 she collected a few of them in the slim volume *Flowering Judas,* which established her critical reputation. The critic and biographer Matthew Josephson, one of Porter's many lovers, brought that work to the attention of his publisher, Harcourt, Brace. Along with the title story, it contained the stories "María Concepción," "He," "Magic," "Rope," and "The Jilting of Granny Weatherall." An expanded version appeared in 1935.

Her relationship with Josephson ended badly—as did all her marriages and love affairs—and before *Flowering Judas* was published she became ill again, as she often did when her affairs of the heart soured. When she was able to get away from her immediate problems, her health almost always improved dramatically. For a time after this particular crisis, in 1929 she lived happily in Bermuda and continued to work on a biography of Cotton Mather, often announced for publication, but never completed. The subject was not a congenial one, and she was not a scholar by temperament. Individual scenes in the published chapters are often well realized, and the writing itself is polished. Had she been writing fiction, not biography, she could have ignored the necessity for historical accuracy and she might then have written a deft satire.

Mexico Again

Porter left Bermuda in the early fall of 1929, and in the spring of 1930 she decided to return to Mexico to work on a novel, never completed, which she was then calling *Thieves' Market*. Soon after she arrived in Mexico, she met Eugene Pressly, a handsome young man thirteen years younger than she. They began an affair that culminated in her third marriage. Though handsome, he often imbibed far too much (as did Porter herself), but he was quiet and reclusive and absolutely devoted to Porter. In *Ship of Fools,* he is presented as David Scott.

During this stay in Mexico, Porter had a traumatic experience with Hart Crane, who did not protect her private life, as had most of her friends. Crane, awarded a Guggenheim fellowship, went to Mexico, where he was invited to stay with Porter and Pressly, who had rented a house. They soon regretted their decision, finding Crane's life-style (his homosexuality was widely known) too excessive for their taste. Finally forced to move, Crane rented the house next door, and his relationship with Porter and Pressly continued to deteriorate. Crane wrote one friend: "It's all very sad and disagreeable. But one imputation I won't stand for. That is the obvious and usual one: that my presence in the neighborhood was responsible for a break or discontinuance of Katherine Anne's creative work. . . . I'm also tired of being made into a bogey or ogre rampant in Mexico and tearing the flesh of delicate ladies. I'm also tired of a certain rather southern type of female vanity. And that's about all I ever want to say about Katherine Anne again personally."[11] Crane's conduct was often outrageous, but he does, in this letter, strip away some of the secrecy around Porter's life and reveal her as her grandmother's child, with a fixed moral code and definite ideas on right and wrong sexual behavior—a stringent code for others, that is, since Porter went her own way in matters sexual and moral. Awarded a Guggenheim fellowship herself, Porter decided to go to Europe. She and Pressly sailed from Veracruz to Bremerhaven on the S.S. *Werra* in 1931. Porter wrote Caroline Gordon a long letter, in the form of a log, about that trip, the fictionalized version of which appeared three decades later as *Ship of Fools*.

Porter and Pressly first went to Berlin, but their quarrels and bickering continued, and he soon left for Spain, either because of the continuing strained relationship or because he knew Spanish and was able to get a job in the embassy in Madrid. Neither of them knew German, but Porter remained in Berlin and made notes about life around her. In later years, she declared that she was aware of the dangers of the Nazis even then. Though that claim was an exaggeration, the published sections of her Berlin journal show that she had some political awareness. She met Hermann Göring at a dinner party and later that night went to a nightclub with him. She apparently met him other times, also, and Givner has suggested that Porter was distressed when he lost interest in her. She did not, as she later fantasized, meet Hitler, and she did not set out to warn the world about the dangers of Hitler and nazism. In fact, she shared at least one belief with the Nazis: anti-Semitism.[12] The exact reasons for her anti-Semitism are complex and cannot be determined precisely, but anti-Semitism was certainly present in the religion of her childhood. Her unhappy affair with Matthew Josephson may have played some small part in the development of her prejudice, but more likely it was mainly due to a general reaction against intellectual Jews she knew in the 1920s. Porter was insecure much of her life, and her anti-Semitism may well have been a manifestation of her social, critical, and intellectual insecurity.

Life in Paris

Porter left Berlin, and after stays in Madrid, Paris, and Basel, she settled in Paris where, no longer a young woman writer from a humble Texas background, she turned herself into a grande dame.

After much indecision she married Pressly, then a secretary at the American embassy in Paris, in 1933. She met Glenway Wescott, Monroe Wheeler, and Barbara Harrison at this time. Many of her acquaintances were now wealthy and aesthetically inclined, and she became far less interested in social issues. During these relatively happy years in Paris, she began to make use of her Texas past and to write or think about the stories concerned with her autobiographical heroine, Miranda, and her grandmother. While in Paris she published two Miranda stories, "The Grave" and "The Circus," and she thought seriously about others that were soon written. Far from her native Texas, she was returning in fiction to the world of her childhood.

Return to the United States

Porter's marriage to Pressly became increasingly more difficult to sustain. She returned to the United States in 1936, and soon completed "Noon Wine," "Old Mortality," and "Pale Horse, Pale Rider." She also began "Promised Land," completed many years later as *Ship of Fools.* After considerable indecision she separated from Pressly in 1937, and he went to South America. That same summer, at the Tennessee home of Allen Tate and Caroline Gordon, she met Albert Erskine, a graduate student at Louisiana State University and business manager of the newly established literary journal *Southern Review.* Her divorce from Pressly came through in the spring of 1938, and her marriage to Erskine took place immediately afterwards. This marriage began disastrously, for Erskine, more than twenty years younger than she, learned Porter's real age the day of the wedding. He was to be her last husband. In 1939 she published three short novels in the collection *Pale Horse, Pale Rider,* and the title story, along with "Old Mortality" and "Noon Wine" are still considered among her best works.

Her fourth marriage, like her first three, was unsuccessful. Porter soon left Erskine and lived a nomadic life, moving restlessly from place to place, never staying anywhere long. She completed more stories, publishing in 1944 *The Leaning Tower and Other Stories,* and she continued to work fitfully at the long novel. For a time she worked as a scriptwriter in Hollywood. She roamed the country lecturing and serving as writer-in-residence at various colleges and universities. She had come to be known as a writer's writer, a southern lady, and a grande dame, and she reveled in her public life, though her private life remained chaotic. Throughout her life, she had long periods in which she was unable to write, and she was often defensive about her writing blocks.

Porter and Herbst

At times, Porter simply moved away from troubled relationships—as she did from her four husbands and from most of her lovers—but in one case she seems to have deliberately betrayed a friend. Beginning in the 1920s she was a close friend of the writer Josephine Herbst. In those early years, both were inclined toward radical politics, though Herbst's commitments were stronger than Porter's. Their friendship later floundered over literary matters— Porter's attack on, and Herbst's defense of, Gertrude Stein, and Herbst's reservations about *Ship of Fools*—but there had apparently been problems before the actual cessation of the friendship.

In *Josephine Herbst: The Story She Could Never Tell* (1984) Elinor Langer makes shocking charges against Porter. Herbst had visited Porter and Pressly for two weeks in their Paris home in July of 1935 and then gone on to Berlin to see for herself what was happening in Nazi Germany. In Berlin, Herbst made contacts with the underground movement and was to write a brilliant series of newspaper articles about her findings. When she returned to Paris, filled with anti-Nazi stories, she found Porter detached and uninterested. Herbst had become more radical over the years and had worked closely with various leftist movements. Porter had, Herbst believed, turned away from politics in the luxury of Paris and had found a haven in apolitical aesthetics. Porter no longer seemed to remember her own apprehensions about the German menace.

In 1942 Herbst had a government job and was the subject of a security investigation by the FBI. Langer introduces the strongest of circumstantial evidence, obtained through the Freedom of Information Act, that Porter denounced Herbst to the FBI, exaggerating and fictionalizing Herbst's involvement in the communist movement. The bizarre stories Porter seems to have told about Herbst represent a malevolence that must shock all of Porter's literary admirers. Langer speculates that Porter, in Reno when the accusations against Herbst were made, was "festering with age" and "must have enjoyed the knowledge that she was doing a foul deed."[13] Other interpretations are possible: Porter, under the emotional strain of another divorce, may not have fully understood the nature of her stories. She may have been overcome by hyper-patriotism brought on by wartime propaganda. It is not now possible to arrive at a final truth about this alleged betrayal.

Final Years

Porter, the loquacious femme fatale of the literary world, kept working on her novel, though she was constantly putting it aside for love affairs, or teaching duties, or because of failing health. Finally, though, when *Ship of Fools* appeared in 1962, it was a great popular success, and for the first time Porter had the funds to live in the grand manner. She enjoyed the adulation, the jewels, the beautiful homes and apartments, but her creative work was virtually over. Her *Collected Stories* appeared in 1965 and won the Pulitzer Prize and National Book Award in 1966. Her *Collected Essays and Occasional Writings* appeared in 1970. With help, she organized her notes about her participation in the Sacco and Vanzetti case, and her rambling account appeared as *The Never-Ending Wrong* in 1977.

Still beautiful in old age, even more talkative, she could be charming when she wished to be, but she was often mean-spirited and vicious. Her assistant, William Raymond Wilkins, a retired naval officer, had been of great help to her in organizing her notes on the Sacco-Vanzetti case, and she dedicated the book to him. Before the book was published, however, she turned against him and when the advance copies arrived, she tore out the dedication page. Her paranoia increased, and she attacked many of those closest to her.[14]

She deteriorated physically and mentally, and in 1980, at the age of ninety, she died. Her body was cremated, and her ashes were buried in Indian Creek.

Her fiction—especially the short stories and the short novels—have earned her the highest critical adulation. Robert Penn Warren has written that many of her stories are "unsurpassed in modern fiction," and he places her in the company of Joyce, Hemingway, Katherine Mansfield, and Sherwood Anderson. Her life was troubled and chaotic, but her fiction imposes order on the chaos of the universe. As she wrote in the introduction to *Flowering Judas,* her stories were mere fragments of a much larger plan on which she was still working, and they should stand as what she was "able to achieve in the way of order and form and statement in a period of grotesque dislocations in a whole society when the world was heaving in the sickness of a millennial change." The fragments she completed were rare achievements by a writer who overcame poverty, lack of formal education, poor health, and a Texas and southern society that actively discouraged her artistic aspirations.

Chapter Two
My Familiar Country

"I write about Mexico because that is my familiar country," Porter explained in "Why I Write about Mexico," a letter to the *Century* in 1923. As a child, she said, she had heard stories about that country from her father, and she had lived briefly in San Antonio, a Mexican-American center. Mexico and its culture had never seemed strange to her.

During the Madero revolution, she viewed a battle between the revolutionists and the federal troops, probably in Juárez in 1911 when she was visiting relatives in El Paso. She most likely crossed the bridge to the Mexican side. After the battle she saw the dead being piled in the public square for burning. An old Indian woman who stood watching with her remarked that the revolution was worth all the trouble because it would bring future happiness—and happiness not of angels, but of people. After this conversation, the political events that followed—the counterrevolution of Huerta and the assassination of Madero; Carranza's revolutionary movement, which resulted in a new constitution providing for badly needed labor, religious, and land reforms; Carranza's assassination in 1920; the coming to power of Obregón's government, which began to institute the reforms of the constitution—all this did not seem false, aimless, or alien to Porter.

Porter told Archer Winsten in an interview published in the *New York Post* on 6 May 1937 that she went to Mexico in 1920 to study art; but, in Winsten's paraphrase of her remarks, she "found herself instead in the center of the Revolution. Being something of a rebel in her own quiet way, it was easy to plunge in on the side of Liberty, Equality and Fraternity. She taught dancing and physical culture in four of the new schools." Much later, in an interview published in the *Paris Review,* no. 29 (1963), Porter spoke of "that wild escapade to Mexico, where I attended, you might say, and assisted at, in my own modest way, a revolution."

Her stories about Mexico, Porter said in the letter to the *Century,* were "fragments, each one touching some phase of a versatile national temperament, which is a complication of simplicities: but I like best the quality of aesthetic magnificence, and, above all, the passion for individual expression without hypocrisy, which is the true genius of the race." Her view of art was a natural outgrowth of this belief, for she felt that the renaissance of Mexican art was natural, not artificial, that it was "unfolding in a revolution which returned to find its freedoms in profound and honorable sources."

Porter's passionate concern for the Mexican revolution was demonstrated in a series of essays that ran counter to the usual cliché-filled, propagandistic attacks on Mexico in the popular American press. In "The Mexican Trinity" (1921) she was explicit in her analysis of the foreign and native enemies of the revolution: the Mexican and American capitalists, the landowners, and the Church—all were subjugating the Indian; the country was in the grip of "Oil, Land, and the Church." The most radical group of revolutionaries, with its many idealists, was tragic because its cause was hopeless; some groups wanted to begin by correcting the most horrible excesses of the old system, but many of the revolutionists merely followed a leader who was intent upon establishing himself in power and not upon bringing about reforms. Porter was acutely aware that the revolution had yet to enter "the souls of the Mexican people," largely because the intellectuals were still writing romances, but also because, even if the intellectuals had cried out against abuses, the Indians could not read. She continued this analysis in "Where Presidents Have No Friends" (1922) with an account of Obregón's attempt to break up the ruling Oil-Church-Land clique and free millions of Mexicans from "poverty, illiteracy, a most complete spiritual and mental darkness."

From these essays, one would imagine that Porter might have turned to propagandistic fiction, but she did not do so. Mexico was the background for her earliest stories, but she did not attempt, through fiction, to offer solutions to the economic and social problems of that country. The very basis of her art was quite different, as she explained in "No Plot, My Dear, No Story": "have faith in your theme, then get so well acquainted with your characters that they live and grow in your imagination exactly as if you saw them in the flesh; and finally, tell their story with all the truth and tenderness and severity you are capable of; and if you have any character of your own, you will have a style of your own; it grows, as your ideas grow, and as your knowledge of your craft increases."

Inside the Mexican Culture

"María Concepción." The first fragment of Mexican cultural life that Porter chose to fictionalize, with truth and tenderness and severity, was that of the still-primitive Indian. The central theme of "María Concepción" (1922) is the strength of life over defeated death, illustrated in María Concepción's treatment of the chickens, in the Indians' unconcern for their buried past, in María Concepción's reasons for murdering María Rosa, and in the protection she is then given by her husband and by the Indian women. [1]

Porter told Enrique Hank Lopez about the germ of the story. She went with her friend the anthropologist William Niven to his excavation site, where she met the Indian woman who became the fictional María Concepción. Niven told Porter about the woman, her husband, and her husband's mistress, and his story was translated almost directly into Porter's short story. According to the account Porter gave Lopez, the real María Concepción had murdered her rival only three months before Porter met her, and Porter said of the beautiful Indian woman: "Here is royalty in every sense of the word." [2]

The opening scene in the story is a brilliant and characteristic performance by Porter, and it demonstrates her complete grasp of technique. María Concepción, wife of Juan, the head digger at the excavations of the buried city, is hurrying down a path that runs through magueys and cactus with their painful thorns and spines, to take noonday food to her young husband and his employer. The heat, the dust, the lonely, forbidding landscape, are superbly drawn, as is María, who is pregnant and walking carefully to keep from stepping on thorns. A proud descendant of an Indian race only partially integrated into Mexican life, she is carrying a dozen live chickens over her shoulder, chickens on the way to market and to death. They peer at her inquiringly, but she gives no thought to them or to their fate.

From the first scene, Porter introduces the reader to the ironic distance between things as they are and as they should be, between truth and fiction, between expectation and fulfillment, between life and art. She lays bare the ambiguities of life; as Robert Penn Warren has aptly remarked, it is irony with a center. María Concepción, hearing and smelling the bees kept by fifteen-year-old María Rosa, feels that if she does not have a crust of honey, her baby will be marked, but what she sees, as she looks through the cactus, marks her baby and María Rosa for death. Peering through the cactus hedge, she can see the golden shimmer of the bees, can hear María Rosa's laughter. She smiles to think of María Rosa's having a man; but, when the man appears, it is her man—a game-cock of a man, flourishing his hat as he goes through the ritual of seduction. She does not interfere; driven by duty, she goes on to the buried city, her ears strumming, as if the bees were in her head, her body burning as if cactus spines were under her skin. The bees and the spines, natural, familiar objects, have instantaneously become sinister, taking on their most painful characteristics.

At first María Concepción wants to die, but not until she has cut the throats of the lovers kissing and laughing under the cornstalks. María Rosa, she thinks, is her enemy, a whore with no right to live; the memory that she herself had struggled even less when Juan had first seduced her is a meaningless fact—for they had later been married in the church.

Before she can go on with her bloody thought, she sees Juan's employer, Givens (a character patterned closely on Porter's friend Niven, with the name barely changed). Givens is perfectly incomprehensible to the Indians, for he is overjoyed at finding in the excavations pottery fragments, bits from painted walls, small clay heads, human skulls—broken pieces from the Indians' buried past. They are puzzled by his delight, for they can make better—and unbroken—pieces of pottery for sale to the tourists. Even so, many of them make what money they have by digging for fragments in the crevasses that crisscross the land like the gashes of a great scalpel.

María Concepción and Givens have no common ground for understanding one another; she regards him condescendingly because he has no woman to cook for him—her concept of what is natural and inevitable in the social order—and he views the Indians condescendingly for "he could feel a fatherly indulgence for their primitive childish ways." He can understand their past but not their present; they are contemptuous of the artifacts of their past and intent only upon their life in the present. For years Givens had been rescuing Juan from various escapades and had often warned him that María Concepción would discover his infidelities, but Givens is unaware of the tensions within María Concepción as she dresses the chicken he selects for his meal, "twisting the head off with the casual firmness she might use with the top of a beet."

Juan does not return to his wife, to the strict young woman who had insisted on a church wedding, but flees with María Rosa, for whom work with the sweet of honey is a way of life. He joins the nearest army, but this Don Juan is more concerned with escape to a more exciting life than with the aims of his commander or whatever cause the army is fighting about.

María Concepción's child dies soon after birth, and she spends long hours in church. Her butchering knife is almost always in hand; Lupe, the medicine woman and godmother of María Rosa, reports, "She is mere stone." When Lupe tells María Concepción that she is praying for her, María orders Lupe to pray not for her but for those in need: "I will ask God for what I want in this world." Later, in avenging herself on María Rosa, she becomes a goddess, decreeing death and taking for her own the newborn baby.

When Juan and María Rosa return a year later, Juan, dressed in the multicolored finery taken from dead soldiers, looks and behaves like a cock. Arrested for desertion, he is saved from execution by Givens. María Rosa gives birth to his son, and Juan, confident that he can manage the two women, stands drinks for everyone at the "Death and Resurrection" pulque shop. Afterward he looks in upon his new son and later in a drunken stupor attempts to beat María Concepción, to become again the master of his household. She resists, even strikes back; and he falls into a drunken sleep.

After refusing to be subdued, María Concepción binds the legs of her dumb chickens as if to go to market, but she does not take the path. She runs stumblingly through the fields—her confused psychological state is objectified in her stumbling and running through the plowed and ordered fields, through the established pattern of Indian agricultural life. She runs unknowingly until at last she regains possession of herself and knows what she wants to do. Her newfound realization is at first shocking, and she sits in the shade of a thorn-filled bush, giving way "to her long devouring sorrow." Sweat pours from her, as if all past wounds "were shedding their salt ichor"—ichor, the ethereal fluid of the gods, is a partic- ularly significant image. Rebozo drawn over her head, her head resting on drawn-up knees, she is a figure of tragedy, consumed by anger and grief. When she rises, she walks calmly, no longer running stumblingly.

It is clear in Porter's story that this seemingly primitive society with its own order, its own morality, its own ethic, has been encroached upon by an alien religion and by the more sophisticated society of the outside world. María Concepción can reestablish order in her world only by breaking outwardly imposed restraints, by becoming a goddess dispensing justice.

The actual murder and the flight of María Concepción are not described; the scene shifts to Juan who is awakened from his drunken stupor by noises he cannot comprehend. María Concepción looms in the doorway, knife in hand, then crawls toward him as she had previously crawled toward a shrine; he was, in fact, a kind of god for her, and she quickly puts away her earlier desire to kill him. Juan at first fears for his safety; but, when he hears her story, he feels immense pride and a desire to protect her. He goes through a carefully reasoned plan of cleansing her and the knife. In a scene set in the dark, then in flickering candlelight, with a heightened sense of nighttime danger, Juan prepares the poor creature, the madwoman as he calls her, for the police. He threatens, in his awakening manly responsibility, to settle accounts with her after she is safe; but she replies, with the charcoal burner casting a yellow glimmer behind the iris of her eyes, that all is settled. Juan knows it is true and wants to repent not as a man but as a child; he cannot understand her or himself, or life itself—life now is confused when once it had seemed simple.

That night they eat from the same bowl, as they had before his flight, symbolizing their reunion; and, when the police come, Juan begins his public defense of his wife. At Lupe's house, where they are taken for the interrogation, the body of María Rosa lies in an open coffin; she is covered with a rose reboza, but María Concepción can see her scarred feet, an image recalling the swollen feet of the death-marked chickens to whom María Concepción had remained insensitive. She is no longer afraid, no longer angry at the pitiable creature in the coffin: "María Rosa had eaten too much honey and had had too much love. Now she must sit in hell, crying over her sins and her hard death forever and ever."

Old Lupe knows the truth but enjoys outwitting the police, her moment of glory. She is intensely aware of the role she plays as medicine woman, a sophisticated position in a primitive society. The police too are aware of the part she is playing, but can do nothing, cannot reorder her primitive justice to fit their own. María Rosa is rejected in death, as the Indians embrace life. María Concepción looks around the circle, and the eyes that meet hers are filled with reassurance, understanding, and sympathy. Absolved, María Concepción takes as her natural right the child who lies at the head of the coffin, new life juxtaposed with the already almost forgotten death. María Rosa, destined for the grave, is to become a part of the buried past.

Juan is destined for life in the dead city. Sentenced to dull, senseless labor, from which he sees no escape, he accepts his fate. He does not understand what has happened to him, feeling only a "blind hurt like a covered wound." Significantly, he does not ponder his fate, but goes to sleep, first throwing off his varicolored clothes, the outward sign of his unfettered life.

María Concepción's world is now aright. She milks the goat, maternally letting the kid suckle briefly, and feeds the baby, who she dreams is hers. Family has won over love; life has won over death.

Joan Givner has rightly pointed out that the theme was a favorite of Porter's: a strong woman triumphs over a weak man after "she acts swiftly and effectively to assert her rights." In addition, Givner notes, Porter is dramatizing her "outrage . . . at the oppression of the Mexican Indian."[3]

Porter introduces in the story a series of opposites: the buried life versus the present, light versus dark, Christianity versus paganism, American versus Indian, love versus duty, walking versus stumbling, honey versus thorns. Constantly shifting from one opposite to another, from one point of view to another, Porter plunges the reader into the amoral-moral world of the Indian, and by extension plumbs the basis of all human existence. In this, her first story, she sees that order is imposed only through reordering or destroying the order-disorder of others.

"The Martyr." The two Mexican stories that follow, "The Martyr" and "Virgin Violeta," are inferior to "María Concepción," and Porter did not include them in her collected stories until 1965. In "The Martyr" (1923) she portrays humorously and ironically an artist who gives himself to self-pity after his model leaves him for another artist.[4] Rubén, the greatest artist of Mexico, while working on a mural, completes drawing after drawing of his mistress Isabel, only to find her taken away from him by her other lover who has sold a painting because it is by coincidence the right color for a wall. Rubén becomes a martyr to love—can think and talk of nothing except the simpleminded girl whose new lover claims he will never make her cook for him and will buy her a pair of red shoes. To ease his pain, Rubén consumes great quantities of food and drink and grows ludicrously fat. A doctor sent by friends prescribes, in a wildly comic scene, diet, long walks, exercise, and cold baths as a cure for the wounded heart; but Rubén can only murmur romantically that Isabel is his executioner, that he will soon be in his narrow, dark grave.

Deserted by his friends, Rubén finally dies of a seizure while dining at "The Little Monkeys" restaurant. The friends, who had fled his tiring stories about Isabel, reappear. The owner of the restaurant confides to the artist Ramón—who is to write Rubén's biography, illustrating it with his own character sketches—that Rubén's last words had been: "Tell them I am a martyr to love. I perish in a cause worthy the sacrifice. I die of a broken heart! . . . Isabelita, my executioner!" Ramón tells the proprietor that the last words "should be very eloquent," for they will "add splendor to the biography, nay, to the very history of art itself, if they are eloquent." The proprietor, who may or may not have heard the final words he quotes, emphasizes that the great artist had been inordinately fond of the tamales served in his restaurant: they were "his final indulgence." The story ends on a note of high comedy and irony: " 'That shall be mentioned in its place, never fear, my good friend,' cried Ramón, his voice crumbling with generous emotion, 'with the name of your café, even. It shall be a shrine for artists when this story is known. Trust me faithfully to preserve for the future every smallest detail in the life and character of this great genius. Each episode has its own sacred, its precious and peculiar interest. Yes, truly, I shall mention the tamales.' "

Darlene Unrue has shown conclusively that the character of Rubén was based on Diego Rivera, the Mexican artist whom Porter knew and with whom she perhaps had a love affair. At first Porter saw Rivera's art as fostering revolutionary ideals in Mexico, but her attitude toward him changed and eventually she came to detest him as a person. Unrue also suggests that Isabel in the story was based on Rivera's first wife, Lupe Marin, and that "Rubén symbolizes the perversion of art to an unholy end. Instead of worshipping at the sacred fount, he is worshipping at the shrine of a human being, a particularly unworthy one, according to the story."[5]

The story is too slight to carry the burden of its irony. It is a mere fragment of Porter's knowledge of the artistic world of Mexico, but it is particularly striking in its limited artistic frame set against the broader context of the Mexican social and economic revolution. It is unfortunate that Porter did not complete and publish more successful stories on the theme of the arts and artists in Mexico, since she was there during the formative stage of the artistic renaissance.

"Virgin Violeta." "Virgin Violeta" (1924) succeeds where "The Martyr" fails, largely because in this story Porter's concern with the characters she portrays is more evident, her descriptions are more vivid, and her meaning is clearer.[6] The title is particularly useful in understanding the story, for, as James William Johnson notes, Porter's titles "almost invariably summarize symbolically the state of affairs she deals with in her story."[7]

Violeta (the color violet is emblematic of gravity and chastity), a fifteen-year-old Mexican girl of good family who has been carefully sheltered by her family and by the Sisters at the convent, sits listening to her cousin Carlos and her sister Blanca read poetry. Violeta is painfully aware of her shyness and unattractive clothes and jealous of her more elegantly dressed, more experienced sister. Blanca, reading the lines "This torment of love which is in my heart: / I know that I suffer it, but I do not know why," seems to Violeta to be anxious to keep the words for herself but they echo Violeta's own emotions—she is tormented by love for Carlos.

In a religious picture of the Virgin Queen of Heaven and St. Ignatius Loyola hanging over Violeta's head, the Virgin "with enameled face set in a detached simper, forehead bald of eyebrows, extended one hand remotely over the tonsured head of the saint, who groveled in a wooden posture of ecstasy." Readers are aware that before his final conversion, Loyola would spend hours thinking of ways to win the favors of a lady, followed by intense periods of spiritual desires. During a vision he saw the Virgin and Son and felt loathing for all his former carnal desires and vowed never again to yield to them. Carlos, as worldly as the unconverted Loyola, stares at the picture, and Violeta notes his "furry, golden eyebrows," his beautiful mouth and chin. Mamacita, like a drowsy cat roused from her sleep, reminds Carlos that he must depart at a reasonable hour, and then she "relapsed into a shallow nap, as a cat rises from the rug, turns and lies down again."

Violeta watches the two readers with "no native wisdom," for at the convent she was taught "modesty, chastity, silence, obedience" and a smattering of French, music, and arithmetic. She sees her life beginning in the future, unrolling "like a long, gay carpet for her to walk upon." The carpet makes her think of a wedding, of coming from the church, but she does not visualize a bridegroom. As befits a virgin, she immediately reminds herself that she does not mean a wedding, she is thinking of a festival; she wants to read about life and love, to be free to read Carlos's poetry without hindrance, without hiding the poems in her missal.

One particular poem that appeals to her schoolgirl romantic notions is about "the ghosts of nuns returning to the old square before their ruined convent, dancing in the moonlight with the shades of lovers forbidden them in life, treading with bared feet on broken glass as a penance for their loves." Violeta, dreaming of life, thinks the poem was written for her, that she was one of the nuns. Her notion of love is an idealization of the Virgin's sacred love.

She sees Carlos through tear-filled eyes, and his face appears soft, as if he had tears on his cheeks. She feels as she often did in church, "enclosed in a cage too small".[8] Silently confessing her love for Carlos, she blushes and prays to the Virgin. When Carlos goes with her to search for his new volume of poetry, she is frightened by the sound of his walk, and stops in the sun room in the moonlight. His hand touches her; she sees his eyebrows hover and swoop as he kisses her. She draws away, and Carlos puts his hand over her mouth to keep her from calling out. She feels intensely ill, for this is not love as she had dreamed it. She threatens to tell her mother, but he insists that it was only a brotherly kiss. She feels she has made a mistake, blushes, and says, "I thought—a—kiss—meant—meant—." But Carlos does not help her, merely says she is young, "like a little newborn calf." When they return to the others, Violeta feels her shame, feels she has acted immodestly. The conflict in her mind over the meaning of love was preordained by her sheltered home life and by the teachings of the nuns. Carlos as worldly Loyola was not part of her immature dream.

When Blanca finds the book, the description of Violeta's emotions demonstrates Porter's great indebtedness to Joyce's *Dubliners*:

"Violeta wished to cry in real earnest now. It was the last blow that
Blanca should have found the book. A kiss meant nothing at all,
and Carlos had walked away as if he had forgotten her. It was all
mixed up with the white rivers of moonlight and the smell of warm
fruit and a cold dampness on her lips that made a tiny, smacking
sound. She trembled and leaned over until her forehead touched
Mamacita's lap. She could not look up, ever, ever again."

Carlos kisses Blanca, since he is soon leaving on a trip to Paris;
when his mouth swoops to kiss Violeta, she sees only his macawlike
eyes and screams uncontrollably. Later, Mamacita tries to be comforting, but Violeta's world has "melted together in a confusion
and misery that could not be explained because it was all changed
and uncertain." She cannot read Carlos' poetry that summer, she
even draws caricatures of him, and she quarrels on more equal terms
with her sister. She cannot settle the questions of love and sex but
when she has to return to the convent in the fall, she weeps and
complains, declaring there is "nothing to be learned there."

Violeta is, in her sensitivity, a prototype of the character of
Miranda, and in her shyness, of Elsa, the plain Swiss girl in *Ship
of Fools,* who, paralyzed with fear, cannot dance with the Cuban
student. The controlled images—the furry eyebrows, the drowsing
catlike mother, the young lovers observed by the inexperienced,
desirous but fearful Violeta, the emblematic picture of the Virgin
and the groveling Loyola, and the tension in the closed room—are
subtly intermingled.

Lopez reported that Carlos was based on Salomon de la Selva, the
Nicaraguan poet whom Porter met in Mexico and with whom she
may have had a love affair. Lopez says she turned against him after
he bragged about seducing the young daughter of one of his friends.
Porter said of him: "I think he was beyond redemption. Yet there
was something strangly compelling about Salomon, a sinister fascination that was not easily resisted. And he certainly knew how to
handle women."[9] In the story, Porter shifts the emphasis from the
man to the girl; of the character Violeta Jane Krause DeMouy notes,
"Like other Porter heroines, she recognizes that she can never love
a man and retain her virtue."[10]

Alienation

"Flowering Judas." "Flowering Judas" (1930) can profitably
be read in the light of "Where Presidents Have No Friends," Porter's

brilliant analysis of the Obregón revolution.[11] Though feeling a profound respect for the aims of the movement, she sees the confusion present at the highest and lowest levels as compounded by foreign opportunists who found support from many groups. "The result," she wrote, "is a hotbed of petty plotting, cross purposes between natives and foreigners, from the diplomats down to the unwashed grumbler who sits in the Alameda and complains about the sorrows of the proletariat. In all this the men in present power are struggling toward practicable economic and political relations with the world." "Flowering Judas" also marks a great change in Porter's fictional presentation of the Mexican scene—for the first time, she presents an extended study of the expatriate in Mexico.

Porter's own account of the composition of this justly famous story provides a key to its meaning:

"Flowering Judas" was written between seven o'clock and midnight of a very cold December, 1929, in Brooklyn. The experiences from which it was made occurred several years before, in Mexico, just after the Obregón revolution.

All the characters and episodes are based on real persons and events, but naturally, as my memory worked upon them and time passed, all assumed different shapes and colors, formed gradually around a central idea, that of self-delusion, the order and meaning of the episodes changed, and became in a word fiction.

The idea first came to me one evening when going to visit the girl I call Laura in the story, I passed the open window of her living room on my way to the door, through the small patio which is one of the scenes in the story. I had a brief glimpse of her sitting with an open book in her lap, but not reading, with a fixed look of pained melancholy and confusion in her face. The fat man I call Braggioni was playing the guitar and singing to her.

In that glimpse, no more than a flash, I thought I understood, or perceived, for the first time, the desperate complications of her mind and feelings, and I knew a story; perhaps not her true story, not even the real story of the whole situation, but all the same a story that seemed symbolic truth to me. If I had not seen her face at that very moment, I should never have written just this story because I should not have known it to write.[12]

Ray B. West wrote in "Katherine Anne Porter and 'Historic Memory' " that he was puzzled by the naming of the central character "because so many of the background facts concerning Laura

were similar to those in Katherine Anne Porter's own experience."
West asked why the character was not named Miranda, and Porter
replied that "Laura was modeled upon a friend" with whom she
taught in Mexico, but the character was a "combination of a good
many people, just as was the character Braggioni."

Later, Porter was to identify the original of Laura as Mary Doherty,
an American Catholic woman who was strongly committed to Mexican revolutionary ideals. Over the years Porter elaborated on the
real-life events incorporated into the episodes of the story, but Thomas
F. Walsh, in one of the best articles ever written on Porter, has
shown that those accounts are not to be trusted. In "The Making
of 'Flowering Judas' " Walsh shows conclusively that the character
and personality of the fictional Laura are a combination of traits
drawn from Doherty *and* Porter; he emphasizes that when she was
first in Mexico in 1920–21, Porter was withdrawn, fearful, and
frigid. Walsh also demonstrates that Braggioni, the corpulent revolutionary, was based on Samuel Yúdico and several other revolutionaries. Porter's childlike faith in the revolution lasted only a few
months, and her alienation from it grew over the years. [13]

Though Walsh has made the definitive statement about the background of "Flowering Judas," it continues to be a favorite story for
symbol hunting. Porter commented pertinently: "Symbolism happens of its own self and it comes out of something so deep in your
own consciousness and your own experience that I don't think that
most writers are at all conscious of their use of symbols. I never am
until I see them. They come of themselves. . . . I have a great
deal of religious symbolism in my stories because I have a very deep
sense of religion and also I have a religious training. And I suppose
you don't invent symbolism. You don't say, 'I am going to have
the flowering Judas tree stand for betrayal,' but, of course, it does." [14]
Porter's statement does underline, in many ways, however, the
validity of much of Ray B. West's interpretation in *The Art of Modern
Fiction*. According to legend, Judas hanged himself from a redbud
tree, and the title occurs in Eliot's "Gerontion," along with the
chestnut and dogwood trees in a sacramental reference. As West
points out, the Judas tree is a symbol of betrayal, and Laura's eating
of the buds is a sacrament of betrayal. Braggioni, the professional
revolutionary, the professional lover of humanity, self-pitying and
ruthless, is ironically presented as a "world-saviour." Eugenio (literally the "wellborn") is somewhat Christ-like; and, like Judas,

Laura is directly responsible for the death of Eugenio since she brings him the narcotics he uses in his suicide.

West's analysis in *The Art of Modern Fiction* of the love symbols in the story was particularly influential in early criticism of "Flowering Judas." He sees Laura as incapable of participating

(1) as a divine lover in the Christian sense, for it is clear that she is incapable of divine passion when she occasionally sneaks into a small church to pray; (2) as a professional lover in the sense that Braggioni is one, for she cannot participate in the revolutionary fervor of the workers, which might be stated as an activity expressive of "love" for their fellow men; she cannot even feel the proper emotion for the children who scribble on their blackboards, "we lov ar titcher"; (3) as an erotic lover, for she responds for none of her three suitors, though she thoughtlessly throws one of them a rose (the symbol of erotic love).

Laura is a wasteland figure, outside religion, revolution, and love. Braggioni, West believes, is capable of redemption, as the foot-washing scene would indicate, but Laura is not, and the theme of the story may be stated: "Only in faith and love can man live."

West, however, tends to overemphasize the religious interpretation. The wasteland-Christian symbolism is, of course, clearly present in the story, and it is used to underscore Laura's disenchantment with what she knows but cannot admit is a false revolution. Without courage to disentangle herself, she drifts along in the movement, is filled with despair, feeds on the lives of others, and realizes the full extent of her betrayal only in her symbolic dream. The dream, utilizing common Christian symbols as it does, indicates the strength of the religious and ethical system she had partially put aside while she worked in the revolutionary movement. True, she sometimes sneaks into church, but to no avail, and she ends by examining the tinseled, jumbled altar with the doll saint whose drawers, trimmed in lace, had dropped about his ankles.

The scene not only reinforces the wasteland theme but also shows clearly that Laura is herself a false revolutionist: she cannot, for example, put aside her aristocratic preference for handmade lace. Braggioni—the name suggests his braggart nature—has also betrayed the revolution, but he can still speak of a world order built anew after the rot of centuries has been destroyed. He speaks of his idealism as if he is addressing followers, boasting of the physical violence and destruction that will come before the new order can flourish. This obscenely fat, false revolutionist, vile as he is, is at least capable of action both revolutionary and amatory; but Laura, although once touched with the idealism of the movement, is now paralyzed, withholding love—even betraying love by throwing the flower to the suitor who stands by the Judas tree.

Laura's involvement in Eugenio's death is clear, but she allows him a final act of self-destruction. Braggioni's attitude is "Am I my brother's keeper?" and he has nothing but contempt for Eugenio—a fool, he calls him. Braggioni is following a completely different set of values from those of Laura, and his concern is for the movement—and his own gratification—not for the welfare of the individual man. Laura has no revolutionary myths deeply implanted in her subconscious, and she sees, in the dream, the implications of her act of betrayal played out in traditional Christian terms. When Eugenio offers his body and his blood, she cries no. Had she subconsciously been able to say yes without reservations, she would have been able to continue believing in the amoral (according to Christian standards) revolution; but in crying no, while knowing that she is, as Eugenio calls her, a cannibal, she realizes for the first time the extent of her betrayal of herself and of her religious, ethical, and humanitarian principles. Some of her Christian precepts are as obviously flawed—her romantic concept of self as Virgin, the hiding of her body, her fear of close human contact, her aristocratic pretenses—but she is unaware of these faults.

Jane DeMouy has argued in *Katherine Anne Porter's Women* that "Laura is her own worst enemy, a woman who, in an effort to protect her integrity, has controlled her emotions to the point of being unable to act according to her own values. In her nightmare, she confronts reality. By refusing to prevent Eugenio's suicide, she has murdered her own principles." Laura is afraid to sleep after her dream of self-realization. That dream, Joan Givner has shown, had a factual basis: it was a transcription of a marijuana-induced hallucination Porter recounted to Lopez. At a party in the summer of 1921 in Cuernavaca, after smoking a reefer, Porter found herself in a state of disorientation: "It was the same room, mind you, but an entirely new dimension of it, the room and all its furniture, curiously detached from its normal rectangular boundaries and now freely floating within itself." She sat talking with her friend Moisés Saenz, who was giving the party, and she told Lopez, "Then with no prelude whatsoever, I had the distinct impression that I could actually see his thoughts whirling around inside his skull, like little levers and springs and tiny cogwheels busily ticking away inside a glass dome." Afraid of all those exposed brains, Porter went on to the terrace overlooking a ravine. As Lopez recounted the incident, Porter, looking beyond the terrace, "could see thousands of shimmering stars caught in the sharp angular branches of a dead and leafless jacaranda tree, and she felt a strong urge to walk out into the dark sky, fully confident that she could indeed defy the laws of gravity." Fortunately she was restrained, and later was able to incorporate the incident into a brilliant piece of fiction.[15]

Porter ends the story on a note of uncertainty, for it is difficult for the reader to believe, given the character of Laura, that this sudden self-knowledge—her insight into her own self-betrayal—will change her significantly. Will her new self-realization frighten her into returning to her religion, a religion that in practice helped enslave the Mexicans? Will she merge Christian idealism with revolutionary idealism and find or found a more worthwhile movement? Or will her newfound knowledge remain useless? Will she continue in her self-isolated, wasteland existence, becoming years later a Mrs. Treadwell in *Ship of Fools,* a middle-aged, alienated figure? Porter provides no answer. Laura had been a victor over self-delusion, but is not her seeming victory also ironic?

"Hacienda." "Hacienda" (1932, revised 1934) was based on a visit Porter made to Hacienda Tetlapayac in July of 1931, just before she left Mexico for Europe.[16] At that hacienda, the Russian director Sergei Eisenstein was making a film, and Porter thought originally that she would write only about her observations of events and people, with the names changed, involved in the filmmaking. Her first version of the story was a thinly disguised fictional account, as was the expanded version published in 1934, but the story she wrote is much more than journalistic reporting. In the revised version, which will be discussed here, Porter continues the wasteland theme of "Flowering Judas." The story has often been misunderstood. Howard Baker, in his review of "Hacienda," found "an inconclusiveness in this story, a lack of a bold theme or of a sturdy fable."[17] Elizabeth Hart in a *New York Herald Tribune Books* review of 16 December 1934 thought the story seemed mere notes for a novel, and Harry John Mooney, Jr., complained that "the narrator has no integral function in the story."[18] A reading of "Hacienda" in the light of Porter's essays and stories on Mexico, the filming of

Eisenstein's *Que Viva Mexico!*, and her 1940 preface to *Flowering Judas* answers many of the objections to what seems to be one of Porter's least popular short novels.

The feudal quality of Mexican society contributes much of the irony in "Hacienda": Uspensky, the Communist film director, has chosen a pulque estate as the site for the filming of a movie, and he uses as actors peons still serving in a feudal system. In actuality, Uspensky bears a close resemblance to Eisenstein, who along with his two assistants was given a leave from the Soviet Union in 1929 to make a movie. After a brief, unsatisfactory stay in Hollywood, they went to Mexico to make the film finally released under the title *Que Viva Mexico!* Upton Sinclair and his wife raised twenty-five thousand dollars for the making of that film. According to Marie Seton, Eisenstein's biographer, much of the actual filming took place at Tetlapayac, a beautiful hacienda owned by don Julio Saldívar. Founded by one of Cortes's followers, the estate had remained in the hands of Saldívar family members after the revolution, "because they agreed to turn it into an agricultural cooperative. Gradually . . . the peons . . . were slowly approaching what might some day become a better life."[19] The peons' future seems forlorn, for in Porter's fictional account an army is present to prevent change.

Eisenstein originally planned to do the movie in six parts, including introduction and conclusion, but only one section, part three ("Novel II—Maguey") was actually distributed commercially in the United States. Worried by the mounting costs of Eisenstein's elaborate film, Upton Sinclair sent his brother-in-law Hunter Kimbrough to oversee the production. Kimbrough, a prudish man, and inexperienced in filmmaking, seems to have antagonized Eisenstein and his followers. Sinclair explained that Kimbrough, "a young Southerner with very old fashioned ideals of honor," considered Eisenstein a great artist, but "I doubt if he had ever heard of such a thing as a homo and he was bewildered to find himself in such company. . . . E[isenstein] wanted money, money, money, and never had the slightest idea of keeping any promise he made. When K[imbrough] obeying my orders, tried the limit the money and the subjects shot, there were furious rows."[20] The Kennerly of Porter's novel corresponds in some respects to the picture drawn of Kimbrough in Seton's book.

Eisenstein's brief script for the Maguey section began with a paean to the maguey, a cactus from which the Indians sucked the juice used in making the alcoholic drink pulque. "White, like milk," he characterized it—"a gift of the gods, according to legend and belief, this strongest intoxicant drowns sorrows, inflames passions." He planned to film the ancient process of pulque making before turning to the Sebastian-Maria story: Sebastian, a peon, takes his bride, Maria, to the hacienda owner as "homage." The guards refuse to let Sebastian enter; and before the owner of the hacienda, who is entertaining friends, can give Maria a few coins, a carriage arrives with his daughter; Maria is forgotten by all except the intoxicated villain who ravishes her. One of Sebastian's friends who sees what is happening runs to tell Sebastian, who attempts to storm the gathering but is repulsed. The distraught Sebastian lusts for revenge, organizes the peons, and makes another attempt to free Maria; but the guards are too strong and the insurgents are forced to flee. They are pursued; and the landowner's daughter, after killing one of the peons, is herself killed. Sebastian is finally captured and summarily executed; the section ends with Maria's finding his body among the magueys. [21]

Using as background the actual hacienda, Porter took a slightly altered version of Eisenstein's artificial plot, and the rather bizarre personalities of those gathered at the hacienda for the filming, and transmuted these materials into fiction. The I-narrator is identified only as a woman writer strangely detached from the events, a disengagement that can be read as an extension of the detachment and isolation of Laura in "Flowering Judas." In "Hacienda," the narrator, like Hemingway's Frederick Henry, distrusts all the old shibboleths, and she seemingly does not attempt to get beneath the surface of the action. She is protecting herself by recording, not probing.

The story begins with a brilliant scene portraying the fastidious Kennerly, the business manager of the movie, in contrast to the docile Mexicans whom he regards as inferior, filthy, disease-ridden nuisances. Always in the background is the "true revolution of blessed memory" that has abolished third-class train travel, just as it has changed the names of many things "nearly always with the view to an appearance of heightened well-being for all creatures." Kennerly, despite his Anglo-Saxon superiority, tellingly describes the graft and corruption of the government, but he is outraged only when personally affected by it.

Andreyev, assistant to the famous director Uspensky, explains to the narrator that the Russians have chosen the hacienda as a setting because the pulque-making process and the hacienda itself are time-less and unchanged. Still shots from the film bear him out: the static land filled with "figures under a doom imposed by the land-scape," the peons filled with "instinctive suffering" but "without individual memory." The camera has caught the "ecstatic death-expectancy which is in the air of Mexico." Andreyev also recounts the tangled affairs of Lolita, the one professional actress in the movie; she first became the mistress of don Genaro, then the inseparable friend of doña Julia, don Genaro's wife. The doña Julia-Lolita lesbian or feigned-lesbian relationship seems perverse and decadent, even in Andreyev's jocularly narrated version.

Much of the story revolves around the various reactions to the tragedy at the hacienda: Justino's shooting his sister. The Indian boy who plays one of the leads in the movie reports that Justino (the Just) had shot his sister accidentally and that, after running away, he had been captured and returned by his friend Vicente (the Victor). One of the peons points out that this was the second time in Justino's family that a brother has killed a child. The song writer Montaña insists that the boy incestuously loved his sister:

> Ah, poor little Rosalita
> Took herself a new lover,
> Thus betraying the heart's core
> Of her impassioned brother. . . .

But Montaña is perhaps more interested in his *corrido* than in the truth, and his version of the events appears no more valid than the others. Kennerly is not concerned with motives but is fearful of a damage suit brought by the parents. Later Kennerly sees the bitter irony of Justino's playing the part in the movie of a boy who by accident kills a girl (played by his sister), attempts to escape, and is captured by the character played by Vicente. Kennerly complains that the dead girl should have been photographed to add more realism to the scene in the movie. When Justino returns, he must play the scene again since the light had not been right the first time. Kennerly with perverted emotions thinks of this prospect with glee.

The narrator is conscious of the spirit of the grandfather, who did not understand or approve of his grandson don Genaro and his wife, and who had retired to a remote section of the hacienda "where he lived in bleak dignity and loneliness, without hope and without philosophy, perhaps contemptuous of both." His grandson lived with even less purpose, giving his life over to women, fast cars, and airplanes, while his wife leads the life of a pampered aristocrat, dressed in the outlandish costumes of a Hollywood designer, and carrying about a foolish lap dog. Don Genaro and doña Julia are Mexican members of the lost generation.

The great Uspensky is enigmatic, dressed in a monkey-suit, with a monkey face, and with "a monkey attitude towards life." He is unconcerned about the fate of Justino; don Genaro is concerned because the judge wants a bribe to release the boy. He will not pay, because to do so would mean continual blackmail by judges. The emotions of Justino and Vicente are hidden from the narrator, but as revealed in their actions their emotions seem more intense in contrast with the insensitivity of those who at first talk endlessly of the affair but then put it out of their minds as "far away and not worth thinking about." The fate of the victimized peon rests with Velarde, "the most powerful and successful revolutionist in Mexico. He owned two pulque haciendas which had fallen to his share when the great repartition of land had taken place." Don Genaro was appealing to him, but Velarde would also demand a bribe.

The heavy, rotting smell hovering over the hacienda from the pulquería is symbolic of the spiritual and moral corruption within the compound and of the corruption in the society itself. "All over Mexico the Indians" partook of the products of the hacienda: they would "swallow forgetfulness and ease by the riverful, and the money would flow silver-white into the government treasury; don Genaro and his fellow-hacendados would fret and curse, the Agrarians would raid, and ambitious politicians in the capital would be stealing right and left enough to buy such haciendas for themselves. It was all arranged."

When the guests visit the pulquería, which is enveloped in religious myths of its own, they see the figure of María Santísima standing in a niche, surrounded by "fly blown paper flowers," a perpetual light at her feet. The walls of the room are covered with a fresco telling the story of this Indian girl who discovered the divine liquor and became a half goddess. Later that day the visitors go to the hacienda chapel but they do not enter; they pose for pictures in front of its closed doors, while Montaña, the poet who is a failure, plays a fat priest. The scene points out again the alienation of all those at the hacienda.

Porter skillfully interweaves the elements of the story—the satiric character sketches, the Mexican social and political scene, the tragic life of the peons, the theme of appearance-reality, which is heightened by the filmmaking motif. The disengagement of the narrator is broken only once, in an incident with dogs. The dogs at the hacienda keep chasing the soldiers to their accustomed place; the dogs also chase the pigs, but the pigs know that they are not in danger and that the chase is actually a game. The narrator sees just before arriving at the hacienda, hungry dogs chasing a rabbit, and cries out, "Run, rabbit, run!" Her Indian driver (unaware that he is symbolically a rabbit, not a dog) shouts encouragement to the dogs and offers to place a wager on the outcome. The fate of the rabbit is not given, just as Justino's fate is not known; but it is likely that neither will survive, a fate particularly meaningful in light of Porter's concern, as stated in the preface to the 1940 edition of *Flowering Judas,* for "the terrible failure of the life of man in the Western world."

"Hacienda" is not slight; it is not the mere notes for a novel. Much more, too, than a comedy of manners, it is a brilliantly executed story of disengagement, of spiritual, physical, moral, and psychological isolation—a short novel of the lost generation. Unlike Hemingway's Jake Barnes and Lady Brett, who can talk about their reasons for being without hope and without faith, the narrator in Porter's story protects herself from the past, does not reveal the reasons for her being an observer instead of an actor, and thereby increases the totality of her isolation.

"That Tree."   In "That Tree" (1934) Porter continues her study of disillusion, this time concentrating on the expatriate colony in Mexico.[22] Here she uses the journalist Carleton Beals and his first wife as models for the story's two unnamed characters—the journalist (Beals) who is telling his story and his companion (Porter?) who is withdrawn, a wasteland figure. The journalist's monologue is interrupted only once, by a quarrel with a newspaperman.

The story is an account of a man's failure to lead the bohemian life of his dreams, of the falsity of those dreams, of the failure of a marriage, the failure of a prim woman to enjoy life or sex—and, by implication, the failure of the Mexican social revolution. The journalist's own words betray him; his listener and the reader see not the ideal life he has dreamed of but the reality behind his words—the fragmentary but sharply defined images of Mexican bohemianism, the American middle classes, American liberal magazines, American expatriates in Mexico, and the codes of conduct of the journalist, his pseudoartistic friends, and his Indian mistress. The narration alternates between heavy irony and biting satire. The unnamed journalist had once had the romantic desire "to be a cheerful bum lying under a tree in a good climate, writing poetry," poetry he knew was worthless, though he insists, too strongly, that he received great pleasure in composing it. His was the fatuous concept of the poet as a poverty-stricken but happily unshackled artist-loafer. After his first wife Miriam left him, he put this dream aside to become an important journalist for liberal American magazines, an authority on revolutions in Latin America, and he confesses to any who would listen that Miriam's leaving him had been his making, that he had become a successful journalist just to impress her.

Miriam, even more than Laura in "Flowering Judas," was prim and proper; she took life seriously. She hated Mexicans and their culture; she held her nose when she went to the market; she refused to have an Indian servant. The squalor, the distance between expectation and reality are all painfully acute to everyone except the narrator, who cannot understand why his wife cried. She hated housework, while he had thought it joyful to wash the colorful pottery outside, with the heaven tree in full bloom. In the three years of their engagement, during which she saved for her dowry, she complained, much like Carol Kennicott in *Main Street,* about the dullness of the Middle West; but, once she saw her husband's bohemian friends in Mexico, she became frightened. She knew they were just waiting for their chance to live proper lives, and she would not believe her husband's mystical insistence that the artist chose poverty. After she left him, he too finally decided that his notions on art, artists, and the artistic life were romantic and impractical.

He had put aside part of his bohemian life to "walk the chalk line" with Miriam, but he found that their chalk lines were different. In a café disturbance she violated his code of conduct. It was just after the Obregón revolution, when four generals came to the city for the installation of the new government: "They infested the steam baths, where they took off their soiled campaign harness and sweated away the fumes of tequila and fornication, and they infested the cafés to get drunk again on champagne, and pick up the French whores who had been imported for the festivities of the presidential inauguration." They quarreled among themselves, reached for their pistols, and when all the Mexican girls on the dance floor swung their escorts to act as shields (the room was "frozen," the music stopped), Miriam hid under a table. She could never understand why he was humiliated; she did not see that she had broken his Hemingwayish code. He broke his own code of conduct when he argued with the newspaperman, but he was too self-centered to be aware of his own failure.

At times, as the drink lowers his defenses, the journalist sees some of the truth about himself, sees that his concept of the artist was romantic; but he can draw no conclusions from his insights other than those of Miriam and the middle classes: success must be tangible, monetarily rewarding, and socially elevating.

Miriam had won. Two wives later, he was taking her back, as mistress, he claims; but his companion knows better. He thought Miriam would now walk his chalk line—he draws a symbolic line on the table cloth, then crosshatches it—but it is he, his companion knows, who would follow Miriam's line. The listener wants to say, "Don't forget to invite me to your wedding," but does not. More deluded than Miranda at the end of "Old Mortality," the journalist says to "the shadow opposite"—an image that continues the waste-land theme of earlier Mexican stories—as they sit in the café now almost emptied, the orchestra leaving: "I suppose you think I don't know—"; then he pauses for effect, "I don't know what's happening, this time," he says, "don't deceive yourself. This time, I know." He admonishes himself as before a mirror. As in "My Last Duchess," the extended monologue reveals the character of a self-deluded, success-failure of a man.

Mooney, in his study of Porter, rather misses the point when he complains that we do not care about the journalist. Porter has used the story of the journalist as a way of dissecting several fragments of American and Mexican culture. The hollowness, the trickery, the chicanery—all are expertly, mercilessly exposed.

From almost complete immersion in Mexican culture in "María Concepción," Porter's artistic attitude toward her Mexican materials changed drastically over the years. Although her essays on Mexico presented frankly the artistic, political and economic changes in Mexico after the revolution, and she did not accept all the changes naively, she at first had high expectations for the country. Forty years later, she tried to explain her changed view of the world and of Mexico. She felt that the evil she described in *Ship of Fools* "wouldn't have happened if any of the people opposed to it had taken hold and not let it happen." In Mexico she had seen "clowns like Hitler" and she realized, on her voyage to Europe in 1931, that "the tragedy of our times is not an accident but a total accident." She considered the voyage "a godsent experience, and yet I wouldn't have been able to see any of these things in perspective if I hadn't first seen them in Mexico. But in Mexico there was always something good about it. In Mexico there was always some chance of salvation."[23]

Porter's later fiction about Mexico, beginning with "Flowering Judas," does not, however, always demonstrate this "chance of salvation," for she turned from the theme of Mexicans in Mexican culture (though, admittedly, she does not idealize the Mexicans in her early stories) to the expatriate, disenchanted, and often disengaged American in Mexico.[24] Thus the movement in the fiction is from inside the Mexican culture to disengagement from it. In the first chapter of *Ship of Fools,* Mexico is treated with great disgust and revulsion. The opening sentence sets the tone for what is to follow: "The port town of Veracruz is a little purgatory between land and sea for the traveler, but the people who live there are very fond of themselves and the town they have helped to make." The "chance of salvation" is not clearly evident.

Chapter Three

The Native Land
of My Heart

During the 1920s and early 1930s, Porter lived in Mexico, Bermuda, Germany, Switzerland, and France. In 1956 she wrote in " 'Noon Wine': The Sources" that those places were "right" and "timely" for her at those times but she confessed that she had not felt at home in any of them. She was continually making notes for stories about central Texas, her part of the South. "I was," she says, "almost instinctively living in a sustained state of mind and feeling, quietly and secretly, comparing one thing with another, always remembering; and all sorts of things were . . . taking on their natural shapes and sizes, and going back and back clearly into right perspective—right for me as an artist, I simply mean to say." These years, spent in what she elsewhere called a "constant exercise of memory," gave the past back to her. Porter's exploration of the past closely parallels the experiences of other expatriates of the 1920s and 1930s who found themselves returning in memory to their native land for subjects to treat in their art.

An evocative passage from " 'Noon Wine': the Sources" captures some of the sights and sounds of Porter's past:

This summer country of my childhood, this place of memory, is filled with landscapes shimmering in light and color, moving with sounds and shapes I hardly ever describe, or put in my stories in so many words; they form only the living background of what I am trying to tell, so familiar to my characters they would hardly notice them; the sound of mourning doves in the live oaks, the childish voices of parrots chattering on every back porch in the little towns, the hoverings of buzzards in the high blue air—all the life of that soft blackland farming country. . . . The colors and tastes all had their smells, as the sounds have now their echoes: the bitter whiff of air over a sprawl of animal skeleton after the buzzards were gone; the smells and flavors of roses and melons, . . . and the sickly sweetness of chinaberry florets; . . . the delicious milky green corn, savory hot corn bread eaten with still-warm sweet milk.

This poetic passage is reminiscent of Mark Twain's recollections of the Quarles Farm in his *Autobiography;* the southern scenes, the smells, the foods are much the same. Porter, just as Mark Twain did, has avoided an Edenic description; she includes the buzzards and the cloying, sickly sweet summer smells ever-present in her shimmering landscape.

Social structure in Porter's childhood was clearly defined. The older generation—those who were products of the South before the Civil War—still ruled. They acted, Porter says in " 'Noon Wine': the Sources," "as if the final word had gone out long ago on manners, morality, religion, even politics: nothing was ever to change, they said, and even as they spoke, everything was changing, shifting, disappearing."

In "Portrait: Old South" Porter provides an account of her grandparents and the vanished past. They had been married in Kentucky about 1850 in a great family ceremony. One of the flower girls, decades later, wrote Porter about the wedding; the ancient lady remembered the great silver candlesticks, the huge cake, the butter dish that held at least ten pounds of butter molded into a floral design, the tremendous wedding dinner. The flower girl lived to boast of the feast, but she, and the others who lived another decade, were destined to eat corn bread.

The Porter family fortunes were depleted by the war, and Porter thinks "the evil turn of fortune" in the grandmother's life made her "truly heroic." Mrs. Porter had no such romantic notions about herself, her granddaughter insisted; she always considered her poverty temporary, and as long as she lived the family never really faced its problems.

Mrs. Porter, her granddaughter wrote, entertained lavishly with the remnants of her finery, spoiled her children and her grandchildren, and punished them erratically and ineffectually.

Though Porter's description of her grandmother's style of life was exaggerated, her grandmother was the most important influence in Porter's early childhood, and her fictional grandmother, Sophia Jane Rhea, seen in Porter's autobiographical Miranda stories, has the mythic qualities of Rhea, the mother of the gods. In these stories

Porter imposes fictional control over the chaos of her early life. They trace Miranda through her early development from "innocent" child to mature, questioning adult.

Grandmother and the Old Order

"The Source." "The Source" (1941), the first story in a series Porter called "The Old Order," is one of a sequence that includes "The Journey," "The Witness," "The Circus," "The Last Leaf," "The Fig Tree," and "The Grave."[1] "The Source" is an introduction to the grandmother and her family and to southern society. Along with "The Witness," "The Journey," and "The Last Leaf," "The Source" provides a fascinating but fragmentary account of the world of Sophia Jane Rhea, a world that helped mold the character of Miranda—just as Catherine Anne Porter and southern society were important in forming Katherine Anne Porter, both as person and as artist.

Early every summer, before the three grandchildren are sent from the town house to the farm, the grandmother begins to think of life at the farm, begins to talk of the change and relaxation soon to be hers, though in fact the change meant great physical exertion and even tighter control over family affairs. Harry, widowed father of the children, takes on an air of patience, masking his "annoyance at the coming upsets and inconveniences to be endured at the farm," for the grandmother represents an authority that could not be challenged.

Although she knows perfectly well she will be a slave driver at the farm, Grandmother Rhea imagines herself walking through the orchard, pruning the rose bushes, training the honeysuckle; just for such occasions, she takes with her a large shepherdess hat that had been woven just after the Civil War, a symbol of the past and her image of herself as she would like to have been. But she never wears the hat, never gives way to her romantic dreams. Instead, she puts on a stiffly starched bonnet, with starch-stiffened, long strings—a visual symbol of her unbending nature and taut control.

She has suffered greatly in her time, and she was vividly reminded of the brutal past every year when the peach tree bloomed outside the town house: she had planted five orchards in three states but now can see only one tree blooming. The peach tree outwardly represents "all her beloved trees still blooming, flourishing, and preparing to bring forth fruit in their separate places."

When she arrives at the farm, accompanied by the other members of the family, Hinry (certainly pronounced and perhaps spelled this way) notices only the grandmother, showing his respect for the source of power at the farm. She thinks of her return as a coming home to the land, to the people, and she immediately sets out, still wearing her widow's bonnet, to inspect the house, the Negro quarters, gardens, barns, and fields. At the Negro quarters, she is told— as she pokes into their belongings, ordering everything to be washed, whitewashed, or varnished—that things are in disorder because of outside work, because of the miserliness of the overseer hired hand. Obviously, she still regards and treats them as if they were still slaves; she soothes their petty or major annoyances, but does not consider making any basic changes in their lives.

Once she turns to the main house, she dusts the sets of Dickens, Scott, Thackeray, Dante, Pope, Milton, Shakespeare, and Dr. Johnson's dictionary—her tastes are standard (do not include American or contemporary authors) and conservative, as her preference for Dr. Johnson's monumental but by then outdated dictionary demonstrates. The whole house is in turmoil—rugs dusted, curtains washed, kitchen straightened—as she busies herself and everyone around her for two weeks reorganizing the farm.

The children have mixed feelings about her; she has been a fixed reality for them since their own mother had died young and she had taken them over, but they also recognized her as a tyrant. No matter how much they love her, they are pleased when she starts making preparations to return to the town house. Miranda does not emerge as a character evaluating the grandmother, and the children's reaction is a collective one.

Signaling the close of her farm visit, the grandmother goes through the ritual of riding her old horse Fiddler again—not the original Fiddler, we learn in "The Journey," but the last in a long line going back to her fifth year. She rides Fiddler to show her strength. He is old and stiff, and she can see the signs of his aging, but she does not admit her own age and infirmities. Then she strolls in the orchard, still not wearing her shepherdess hat, to make final improvements here and there, missing nothing.

Realizing that the town house is by now in a state of disorder, she hastens back to restore it again. Her greatest delight is in imposing what is essentially an unnatural order on everything around her. The cycle never ends: disorder to be ordered, but disorder always multiplying, never to be conquered.

Taken alone, the story is a remarkable portrait of a strong-willed southern woman. Seen as the introduction to the Miranda stories, it is even more effective. One sees the grandmother's power and control over family and farm and that the grandmother is herself the source of the strengths and weaknesses of the whole Rhea family.

"The Witness." The grandmother has many connections with the past—her horse Fiddler, the shepherdess hat, her lost orchards—but the children get another limited glimpse of the past from Uncle Jimbilly, formerly a family slave. In "The Witness" (1944)—discussed here out of sequence since the grandmother is still alive—we learn that he does odd jobs about the farm, and that, if asked correctly, he would carve tombstones to be placed on the graves of the dead birds and animals buried by the children.[2] They go through elaborate burial ceremonies, acting out no doubt their ever-present, yet uncomprehending, awareness of the death of both humans and animals. While Uncle Jimbilly carves the grave marker, he tells long ghost stories that the children do not understand—had he seen the ghost? was it a ghost or a man? He is a master storyteller, but his narrative technique, like James's in "The Turn of the Screw," is one of ambiguity, leaving unanswered questions for the children to ponder.

Generally, Uncle Jimbilly talks of the brutalities inflicted upon the Negro in slave times: "Dey used to take 'em out and tie 'em down and whup 'em," he would mutter, "wid gret big leather strops inch thick long as yo' ahm, wid round holes bored in 'em so's evey time dey hit 'em de hide and de meat done come off dey bones in little round chunks." Then he would tell of corn shucks being put on their backs, and set afire, and of vinegar poured over the staunched wounds. The children cannot quite believe his accounts of slavery—they know he was not tortured because he belonged to Sophia Jane—but the stories make them nervous. They are hearing a mythic, violent presentation of the life of a southern Negro, getting a glimpse of slavery both distorted and accurate. The accounts of slavery they hear from their elders collide with Uncle Jimbilly's stories. Which should they accept, which reject? Uncle Jimbilly is cantankerous and religious—no, he would not carve "Safe in Heaven" as an epitaph for a tame jackrabbit—but he lacks authority, not because he is an ex-slave, but because he adopts a role the children can see through. When exasperated with the children, he would threaten to skin them alive, to pull their teeth to make a new set for the tramp, Old Man Ronk; but he never gets around to doing these things. His threats of violence are obvious and exaggerated, and "even the most credulous child" is not frightened by them.

The children in this story are given names and ages, and their characters begin to emerge: Maria, ten, is "prissy"; Paul, eight, is "sad-looking"; and Miranda, six, is "quick" and "flighty." The story takes on meaning from its place in the sequence of all the Miranda stories, because here we learn of the children's early years. More important, the children are learning to evaluate the testimony of a witness to the past, a witness whose testimony runs counter to other stories of their southern legacy and to the family myths about it.

"The Journey." "The Journey" (1936) sketches in the whole life span of the grandmother and ends with her death and the impending new order.³ Moving back and forth in time, the story begins with her last years, when she sits with the ex-slave Nannie, talking endlessly about the past, institutionalizing and protecting it. The attitude of the children is clearly stated: they are faintly embarrassed by their grandmother's old-fashioned ways. The two old ladies, their lives intertwined since Sophia Jane was five— Nannie's age and birthdate are unknown, but Sophia Jane had provided her with both a year and date of birth—sit with the scraps of past finery, making patchwork coverings for such possessions as a functional rolling pin hewn by a famous pioneer ancestor. As they sew, they cover the past with the finery of their talk. Even the future seems a repetition of their past: "They would agree that nothing remained of life as they had known it, the world was changing swiftly, but by the mysterious logic of hope they insisted that each change was probably the last; or if not, a series of changes might bring them, blessedly, back full-circle to the old ways they had known." Actually, the past had been bitter for them both; the grandmother in her authoritarian role had attempted but failed to keep her world stable; Nannie had been assigned a place in that world with no choice but always to obey.

Sophia Jane's father had bought Nannie and her parents in 1832; at the same time he had bought a pony, the original Fiddler, for

Sophia Jane, but she had demanded to be given also the little potbellied Nannie, seemingly so worthless that she had been sold for twenty dollars by a family emigrating to Texas. The sale, the crowds, the events of the auction seemed, decades later, almost mythic to Nannie; but she was horrified, when at the wedding of one of the grandmother's granddaughters to a grandson of Nannie's original owner, the old gentleman mentioned to Nannie her low price. Emancipated, Nannie still measures her worth, at least partially, by the monetary standards of slavery.

The grandmother, married to her cousin Stephen, a weak man, a dissipator of her fortune, is contemptuous of men. After the death of her husband, she moved the family to Louisiana to take over a sugar refinery, but saw that she could not manage it. She then sold it at a loss to move to the central Texas land her husband had bought years before. (Since Mr. Porter died in Texas, after living there many years, these events are not true; for personal and artistic reasons Porter emphasized the matriarchal aspects of her fictional family.)

The grandmother's feelings are the important ones and not to be tampered with; her opinions are always correct. Her children grew up and married, and she helped them establish homes, but they fled her domination. She finds fault in everyone: Miranda's mother, she insists, had been too delicate, a failure as a housekeeper, and could not bear children successfully.

Just as she is beginning to work on the faults of the orphaned children, Sophia Jane dies. Characteristically, at this moment she is trying to set disorder aright, or rather what she deems disorder in the household of a son and daughter-in-law. Completely ignoring the wishes of the young Mrs. Porter, Sophia Jane is busy reorganizing the garden, a task that calls for moving a fifty-foot adobe wall, when she announces how well she feels, and falls dead. With her death, we learn in other Miranda stories, the family rapidly begins to come apart, for the grandmother's power in the family is both actual and mythic. The family's strongest connection with the dead weight of the past is severed; it now has no real direction to follow. The extent of the change is explored briefly but poetically in the following story.

"The Last Leaf."   A fitting close to the first section of the family chronicle, "The Last Leaf" (1944) is the elderly ex-slave Nannie's story.[4] After Sophia Jane's death, Nannie, old and decrepit herself, surprises the family by moving away from the family house to a small cabin, which is symbolically across the creek. The children try to assure the old woman that they love her, but she really does not care; her ties are with the past, and she is now ready for her own death. The world of the Rhea family is changing: "the old world was sliding from under their feet, they had not yet laid hold of the new one."

The family needs Nannie as servant and matriarchal figure. She would return to them briefly, accept their gifts (offered as bribes that she might return permanently); but she always goes back to her own cabin and her new independence. Uncle Jimbilly, her husband of convenience, tries to return to her; but she would not, she says, spend the rest of her life waiting on him: "I've served my time, I've done my do, and dat's all." She is repeatedly described in terms of African nobility, and it is clear that in rejecting the present, she is returning not to her past with grandmother Rhea but to an African tribal past—a regal historic past.

Nannie is to the Rheas a firm tie to their own past, and she manages to control Harry by insisting that she had suckled him, though we learn in the story that she had been a wet nurse for the elder Rhea children, but not to Harry. Nevertheless, Harry always gives in to "the smothering matriarchal tyranny to which he had been delivered by the death of his father. Still he submitted, being of that latest generation of sons who acknowledged, however reluctantly, however bitterly, their mystical never to be forgiven debt to the womb that bore them, and the breast that suckled them." In this brief passage, Harry's essential weakness is subtly probed; like his father, he allows women to dominate. Like her former owner Sophia Jane, Nannie dominates the men in her life. Though Nannie's control was not to endure, she does, in Porter's story, take on permanence, just as the leaf in O. Henry's story lasted because it was painted on the wall. Porter avoids the trick ending of the O. Henry story, just as she avoided the easy moral of Oliver Wendell Holmes's poem:

> And if I should live to be
> The last leaf upon the tree
> In the spring
> Let them smile as I do now
> At the old forsaken bough
> Where I cling.

Miranda the Child

The four stories that follow are arranged in approximate narrative chronological order, not in the order of their composition, to allow a clearer presentation of Miranda's discovery of and initiation into the world. These stories, among Porter's finest, are complex, subtle probings by the sensitive Miranda as she tries to find her way in a world far different from the seemingly stable universe of Grandmother Rhea.

"The Fig Tree." Jesus saw Nathanael coming to him, and saith of him, Behold an Israelite indeed, in whom is no guile!

Nathanael saith unto him, Whence knowest thou me? Jesus answered and said unto him, Before that Philip called thee, when thou wast under the fig tree, I saw thee.

Nathanael answered and saith unto him, Rabbi, thou art the Son of God; thou art the King of Israel.

Jesus answered and said unto him, Because I said unto thee, I saw thee under the fig tree, believest thou? thou shalt see greater things than these.

And he saith unto him, Verily, verily, I say unto you, Hereafter ye shall see heaven open, and the angels of God ascending and descending upon the Son of man. (John 1:47–51)

The character of Miranda in "The Fig Tree" (1960), is a Miranda with a particular, tangible past, a product of the Lost Cause and its aftermath, a true granddaughter of Sophia Jane.[5] Porter's use of the name Miranda came by way of her ardent (and fickle) suitor of the middle 1920s, Francisco Aguilera, who began a letter to her, "Ariel to Miranda: Take this slave of music for the sake of him who is a slave to thee!" It is safe to assume that Aguilera knew Porter was familiar with Shakespeare's *Tempest,* though curiously enough in 1958, Porter ascribed the line and the name to Shelley.[6]

As Edward Greenfield Schwartz pointed out in "The Fictions of Memory," Porter's Miranda begins her journey where Shakespeare's heroine ends hers. Shakespeare's Miranda cries out:

> O, wonder!
> How many goodly creatures are there here!
> How beauteous mankind is! O brave new world,

That has such people in't.

(5. 1. 181–84)

Shakespeare's Miranda is too sheltered to know that her belief in beauty and nobility is largely deceptive, and she has too little experience to understand Prospero's answer, " 'Tis new to thee." Shakespeare uses the name Miranda in the Latin sense of strange and wonderful, but Porter added the Spanish meaning—"the seeing one"—for in the later stories Miranda has the ability to see through the shams of her society and her training. In "The Fig Tree" she sees her grandmother and Aunt Eliza clearly, realizing, because of her watchfulness, many of the absurdities of the adult world.

"The Fig Tree," finished in Bermuda in 1929, was to have been included in *The Leaning Tower* collection but Porter misplaced the manuscript, and it was lost for many years. When she finally rediscovered it, the story was published in *Harper's Magazine* in June 1960. A note accompanying it in *Harper's* refers to it "as the last of the Miranda stories."

The story seems to have as its literary background Blake's *Songs of Innocence and Songs of Experience,* with their dramatic use of " 'weep! 'weep!,' " but Porter goes far beyond the chimney-sweep poems when she uses these key words in "The Fig Tree." Though she appears to be deeply indebted to Blake's imaginary world, it is characteristic that her borrowings are completely integrated into her own special fictional world; they are not extraneous quotations nor paradings of erudite knowledge.[7]

"The Chimney Sweeper" poem in *Songs of Innocence* begins with an explanation—the sweeper's mother had died when he was young, and his father had sold him when he could barely say " 'weep!" He consoles his companion Tom, whose curly white hair had been clipped, saying that the soot would not now spoil the hair. That night, Tom dreams of thousands of sweepers locked in "coffins of black" released by an angel, running across the green plain, washing in the river, and finally ascending. The angel tells Tom that if he is good, God will be his father and he will never be without joy. When Tom wakens, he is happy and believes that "if all do their duty, they need not fear harm."

In *Songs of Experience,* however, the chimney sweeper cries " 'weep!" while his parents are in church. Because he had been happy on the heath, his parents had put him into "the clothes of death" and taught him to sing "the notes of woe." He concludes,

> And because I am happy, & dance & sing,
> They think they have done me no injury,
> And are gone to praise God & his Priest & King
> Who make up a heaven of our misery.

From the beginning of Porter's story, Miranda is shown between the states of innocence and experience. She is first seen struggling with Aunt Nannie who is combing her hair. Aunt Nannie, following Harry's order, draws the hair back and puts a band around it, an act similar to the cutting of Tom's hair. Nannie firmly attaches a bonnet that the father insists Miranda wear; Miranda's face must not be spoiled with freckles. Grandmother, Harry, and Nannie, all restrict Miranda's innocent joys, by their very acts pushing her toward knowledge while attempting to keep her pure, that is, keep her skin unblemished. The restrictions of the elders are symbolically similar to those imposed by the parents of the child chimney sweepers in *Songs of Experience.*

As the family is preparing to leave on a summer day for the family farm named Cedar Grove, Miranda asks if they are going to "Halifax"—she knows her father Harry calls it "Halifax," because it is hot there, but she is unaware of the slang meaning of the word. Her Grandmother Rhea admonishes her and tells her to call things by their right names, but Miranda notices that Harry does not call the grandmother by her correct name: she was not "Mammy" or "Mama." These thoughts lead to thoughts of death: "Mamma was dead. Dead meant gone away forever. Dying was something that happened all the time, to people and everything else. Somebody died, and there was a long string of carriages going at a slow walk over the rocky ridge of the hill towards the river while the bell tolled and tolled, and that person was never seen again by anybody." This scene, which is also archetypal, is an accurate reproduction of the Indian Creek landscape, except that the funeral procession for Mrs. Porter would have gone from the house on the river, across the rolling hills, to the church, and then to the cemetery. Miranda's literal concept of death, her acceptance of its naturalness, stems from her acceptance of the cycle of birth and death in both animals and humans. But to her natural feelings are added the rituals of death she has learned from the death of her own mother and of neighbors and relatives.

Before leaving for the farm Miranda finds a dead chicken in the fig grove, and she immediately begins the adult-learned ritual of burial, selecting a shoe box of the right size and attempting to make the partially grown chicken as attractive as possible. The fig has several connotations in the story in addition to that seen in Jesus' statement to Nathanael. After Adam and Eve fell from their state of innocence, they covered themselves with aprons of fig leaves; the fig grove was a dark and shady place, and in many mythologies groves or dark forests are often connected with evil; and the fig is often a symbol of the womb.

Miranda has to hurry with her preparations for the burial, for if she is discovered getting the box she will have to explain and that will ruin the spontaneity and joy of the act. Just after she makes a mound over the grave, a mound just like that on human graves, she hears a strange sound, "weep, weep, weep." In her state of innocence she has made no distinction between animal and human life, affording the chicken a childlike version of a southern, Christian burial. The sound "weep" makes her think she has buried the chick alive, although she knows perfectly well how to tell when animals are dead.

Foiled from digging into the grave to see if the chicken is dead, for the Rhea party is ready to leave for Halifax, Miranda begins to cry but cannot and will not explain why she is crying. The adults are, as usual, uncomprehending (Grandmother Rhea could not even tell the difference between town and Halifax figs), and the father thinks Miranda is having a tantrum because she has left a doll behind. He has not discovered that Miranda is not interested in inanimate things; she loves live things (doll clothes were fun to put on kittens who tore them off). It is the promise of forty kittens at Cedar Grove (Harry calls it by its proper name) that finally calms Miranda; as in "María Concepción," life triumphs over death.

At Cedar Grove, they join Great-Aunt Eliza, an amateur scientist, who with Hinry as assistant puts her telescope up on the hen house. Dressed in snuff-colored clothes, with snuff-colored eyes and iron-gray hair looking like a wig, Eliza—gathering specimens, wielding both telescope and microscope, quarreling with Sophia Jane—is a remarkably complex and comic figure. Her name reminds us of Eliza in Joyce's "The Sisters." Miranda's reactions toward her are again colored by both innocence and experience. Miranda accepts her as part of the Halifax world, but she rejects the snuff-flavored gumdrop by washing it and the smell away (a parallel to the boy's refusal of biscuit in "The Sisters").

Miranda learns more about the adult world when she sees Eliza and Sophia Jane bickering. Like Shakespeare's Miranda, Porter's character watches and listens carefully "for everything in the world was strange to her and something she had to know about." She sees that Sophia Jane and Eliza are proud of having children and grandchildren, and that they knew exactly what children were to do in every situation, but when she sees them arguing just as she and Maria did, she becomes "a little frightened" and begins to move away. She also learns that the grandmother's strict social standards are not always as stringent as they appear, for Sophia Jane speaks of snuff-dipping as a lower-class habit but ignores her own sister's addiction to it. The grandmother's rules for table manners are inconsistent also; the children are not allowed to play at the table, but Eliza brings her scientific specimens to dinner. Eliza's approach to science is religious: she sits over her experiments "as if she were saying her prayers," an attitude that closely parallels that of the praying parents in Blake's poem.

The night Eliza allows the children to gaze at the stars, she has to admit that science does not have all the answers. Miranda, upon seeing the moon, cries out, "Oh, it's like another world!" But, when she asks if the millions of other worlds were the same as earth, Eliza replies, "Nobody knows, child." Miranda sings, "nobody knows," in her head, dazzled with joy, accepting the mysteries, filled with expectations, still in her state of blissful innocence.

Returning to the house on the dewy path through the fig grove, Miranda smells the leaves and touches one for luck. Then she hears the "weep" sound again and cries out in fright. Eliza explains that the sound is only the tree frogs, but her simple answer offers Miranda a new mystery: if this sound comes from the first frogs of the season, how had Miranda heard them earlier in another fig grove?

Though Eliza's accuracy is in question, Miranda trusts her answer: " 'Thank you, ma'am,' Miranda remembered finally to say through her fog of bliss at hearing the tree frogs sing, 'Weep weep . . . .' " But, one can properly ask, will the scientific answer be enough for Miranda? It has allayed one fear, but it has not explained the mysteries of life and death. She has accepted an explanation which is, in fact, based on a single vision of life. Even the narrator distrusts the implicit trust of Miranda, for Miranda is in a "fog of bliss." The mist perhaps hides other questions, other answers. In "Pale Horse, Pale Rider," Miranda, like Nathanael, is to see "heaven open."

"The Circus." The young Miranda in "The Circus" (1935) is seen along with her family and visiting relatives, a motley lot, already inside an enormous circus tent, a microcosm of the world.[8] At first Miranda feels comfortable. Looking down under the plank seats, she sees little ruffians staring up at her. (The scene is similar to the later passages in *Ship of Fools* in which the first-class passengers peer down at inmates in steerage.) One whispers and nudges another, and Miranda asks Dicey what they are doing. Dicey looks, draws her knees together, and admonishes Miranda to "stop throwin' yo' legs around that way." Miranda is unaware of the sexual meaning of Dicey's admonition, but she feels uncomfortable.

The little girl's initiation into the horrors of the world comes immediately. She cries out in panic at the blaring band, the smells, the colors, and closes her eyes against the scene. Laughter from the audience is deceptive; she opens her eyes and sees a frightening clown with a whitened face, tufted eyebrows, and scarlet mouth painted in a perpetual grimace. Miranda thinks he is walking on air or flying, but when she sees he is walking on a thin wire, she is terrified[9] by his feigned falls, his comic flirtations with death, clinging to the wire with one leg, the other waving about like a giant insect feeler. (Charles Kaplan has pertinently observed that animal and insect imagery is used to describe humans in this story and human images used to describe animals.) The sensitive Miranda cannot bear the audience's shrieking and laughing "like devils in delicious torment." She screams and cries and is sent home with Dicey. Grandmother Rhea, who disapproves of circuses, sits watching the spectacle with her veil only half raised.

As Miranda is being carried out, she sees a dwarf dressed as a gnome, staring at her with inhuman eyes (he is an early study of Herr Glocken in *Ship of Fools*). She strikes at him, sees his adult look of displeasure, realizes he is human, and is newly afraid. Within the circus tent Miranda saw obscene sexual leers, craven pandering to the audience's desire for mordant humor in the parody of life-death played out on the high wire, and adult disapproval in the eyes of the misshapen dwarf.

Miranda encounters repeated displeasure and disgust through the day. Dicey grumbles all the way home about missing the circus, but she is careful not to go too far, for she is a Negro servant and understands perfectly her limited freedom to disapprove. When the family returns, the other children describe the circus in detail, sympathize with Dicey, and look accusingly at Miranda; there is malice in their eyes as they torment her. Harry, knowing his mother's dislike of circuses, remarks that no harm has been done, but Grandmother Rhea, echoing Blake, says: "The fruits of their present are in a future so far off, neither of us may live to know whether harm has been done or not. That is the trouble." She can understand partially the reactions of the child Miranda, but she cannot communicate with her, cannot ease her pain. The father, uncomprehending and insensitive, even asks Miranda what good it had done her to miss the circus, at which she cries again, whereupon she and her supper are sent to her room.

Miranda tries to imagine that the circus is what the other children think it, bright and colorful and fun; but, when she falls asleep, all her inventions flee, and she sees only the terrified face of the clown falling to his death and the grimace of the dwarf. She screams in her sleep, trying to scream away the torments of the day. Dicey threatens to spank her, and Miranda, who usually announces that she minds only her grandmother, is too afraid to talk back. She begs Dicey not to be angry, to stay with her, and to leave the light on.

Collecting her Christian charity, Dicey controls her exasperation and tries to soothe the child. But her message, outwardly calming, is as false and deceptive as the circus scenes: "Now you jes shut yo eyes and go to sleep. I ain't going to leave you. Dicey ain't mad at nobody . . . *no*body in the whole worl'. . . ." Porter captures in this brief story much of the horror and human destructiveness she later deals with in *Ship of Fools*.

"The Grave." The action of "The Grave" (1935) is set in a frame important for an understanding of the story. [10] The first paragraph deals, in a restricted way, with family history, compressing much of our knowledge of the Rheas into comments about the many moves of the grandfather's body. Grandmother Rhea had moved the body first to Louisiana, then to the family burial ground on the farm, and as the story opens in 1903, it is being moved to the public cemetery. The last paragraph, recounting a scene almost twenty years later, comments on and extends the significance of the story.

The two scenes within the frame are seemingly simple. The children Paul and Miranda are on their way hunting when they stop to play in the empty grave of their grandfather; Paul finds a ring there and Miranda a dove-shaped screw head from the coffin. After leaving the burial ground, Paul shoots a rabbit about to give birth, and for the first time Miranda understands the process of birth. The point of view—sometimes swooping close to Miranda, entering into her mind, recording her feelings and emotions; at other times withdrawing into objectivity; and sometimes shifting to Paul, portraying him in more depth and also giving the reader another view of Miranda—is particularly skillful.

In a blinding hot sun the two children enter the burial ground; they are both awed and fascinated when they see the graves. At the age of nine, Miranda is still largely innocent, seemingly little influenced by the knowledge gained earlier in "The Fig Tree" and in "The Circus." With the coffin gone, the grave is merely a hole in the ground, and she leaps into it, scratching about as if she were a young animal. The earth has a pleasant, corrupt smell, and she finds a silver dove with a deep cleft in its breast, a flawed symbol of peace and innocence—the grandfather's body had found no peace and now Miranda's innocence is about to be shattered. Paul finds a ring, a gold band, probably a wedding ring, engraved with flowers and leaves, fertility symbols. The two children trade treasures, and Miranda wears the ring on her thumb, literally because she is young and it fits there, but symbolically she is not yet ready to wear such a band on the correct finger.

The children then flee the cemetery, for the land is no longer theirs, and they are afraid of being caught trespassing. They continue their hunting expedition, squabbling over shooting rights; Paul claims the right to shoot first if they see a rabbit or dove, and Miranda asks idly if she can fire first if they see a snake.

Immediately after this Biblical and Freudian imagery, Miranda transfers her interest from shooting to the gold ring on her thumb. She is then dressed asexually in hired-man's hat, thick sandals, and overalls, the wearing apparel she prefers, since she has had no feminine stirrings and since her father does not object—it saves her dresses for school. Looking at the ring, she suddenly wants to return to the house, bathe, dust herself with violet talcum powder, and put on her most feminine dress. On a deeper level she shares her grandmother's yearning for the family's lost luxury and grandeur, and she envisions herself dressed in finery in this fantasy world.

Before she can return to the house, Paul shoots a rabbit and begins to dress it. Miranda admires her brother's skill in skinning rabbits, and she often has Uncle Jimbilly tan the skins to make fur coats for her dolls. She does not enjoy playing with dolls, but she has been taught that luxurious tastes, like fur coats, are rightfully hers, and she is then too innocent to see the connection between the destruction of the fur-bearing rabbit and the fur coat, between slavery and the antebellum family plantations, just as she cannot see that the "dark scarlet, sleek, firm" flesh of the rabbit is now prematurely destined to decay.

In the dead body of the rabbit the children find unborn babies, each one enveloped in a "scarlet veil." Paul removes the membrane, and they see each tiny thing clearly, with down "like a baby's head just washed," and Miranda knows instinctively and instantly the process of birth. Paul buries the babies in the mother, wraps her in her skin, hides the body in the sage brush, swearing Miranda to secrecy, for he does not want his father to think he is introducing her to things she should not know.

Miranda, true to her newfound knowledge, does not tell and finally puts the incident into the grave of her mind. Almost twenty years later, in a Mexican market, she comes across the same smells of decay and a tray of sugar sweets, some in the shape of tiny baby rabbits, plunging her into a Proustian recreation of the long-forgotten childhood scene. She can smell in the market—which by extension becomes the world just as the circus arena does—the remembered scents of sweetness and corruption she had smelled long ago, scents that bring to mind the incidents and knowledge she had gained that day. In the midst of teeming life and rapid decay, confronted by the Indian vendor with his visible symbols of fertility, Miranda sees clearly the implications of those almost forgotten incidents.

Through this concluding frame all the themes of the story are brought together, and it is clear that Porter means to show what Miranda has learned—that life is doomed to death, but that one's reaction to this knowledge is important. At first, Miranda is horrified when she remembers the grave and the rabbit; her reactions to death were quite different from those of her grandmother, who was possessive, who moved her husband's body, and who planned a conventional, late Victorian burial ground. The father did not discuss such things as the connections between birth and death, and Miranda's new knowledge had to be kept secret from him. Paul had seemingly known about birth all along but had not told her. Her vision in the market reveals to her that long ago she had learned that life is subject to corruption and death, that life builds on other life and on death, and that the world is filled with chaos, disaster, and destruction.

As her horrible vision fades, she sees her twelve-year-old brother still standing in the blazing sun, smiling soberly, turning the flawed dove in his hands. This second image in the market is a return to the symbol of the flawed innocence of her brother Paul, who had inadvertently destroyed a part of her own innocence.

The corruption-filled market in a strange city of a strange country dramatically highlights the wandering journey of Miranda, who cannot accept family legend, cannot live in family tradition (we learn in "Old Mortality"), and finds herself an alien in a corrupt world.

"Old Mortality."   The title "Old Mortality" (1938) is probably from Sir Thomas Browne's "Urne-Burial."[11] The burial urns show "old mortality, the ruines of forgotten times, and can only speak with life, how long in this corruptible frame, some parts may be uncorrupted; yet able to out-last bones long unborn, and noblest pyle among us." Porter owned a copy of a 1921 edition of Browne's *Religio Medici and Other Writings,* which contains these lines.[12] Although Porter denies having read Sir Walter Scott's *Old Mortality,* in "The Source" the fictional family has a set of Scott's works. Scott's novel begins with a description of John Paterson, known as Old Mortality, a religious enthusiast who wanders the Scottish countryside, caring for the graves of Covenanters killed by the last two Stuarts. He seeks out obscure graves, cleans moss from the stones, renews the inscriptions, and repairs the emblems of death. He thinks he is fulfilling a sacred duty, and superstition has it that gravestones he renews will not decay again. On a symbolic level, Miranda cleanses the past just as Old Mortality renewed the stones.

In her biography of Porter Joan Givner has shown that Porter incorporated into her family legend stories she had heard recounted by her Aunt Ione, wife of Harrison's younger brother. Ione had been educated in a New Orleans convent. She had beautiful clothes

and jewels; she had lived a life quite different from that of the
Porters in their cramped four-room house in Kyle, and she was
idolized by the young Callie. Givner has also shown that when
Porter went to Bermuda in 1929 she lived for a time at Hilgrove,
the kind of spacious mansion in which she would like to have been
born. She incorporated the fine old china, the furnishings, and the
library of Hilgrove into her fictional past.

Porter's short novel begins on a note of ironic contrast between
beauty and impermanence. Both Miranda and Maria hear adults say,
"How lovely," on seeing the photograph of Amy, who is now dead.
True, her picture shows a spirited-looking woman, but she is
caught in the "pose of being photographed, a motionless image in
her dark walnut frame." The background of the picture seems faded
and Amy's costume appears old-fashioned, like the finery much
loved by Grandmother Rhea.

In "Part I (1885–1902)," the children hear the family legends
about Amy (literally, "the beloved"), and while the children are
observant enough to see that some details of the legend are untrue,
they go on believing in them. The naive Miranda even believes that
Mary, Queen of Scots, died on stage the night of the performance.
Obviously, then, Miranda could believe that romantically con-
sumptive Amy would toy with Gabriel's affections, would inspire
men to fight over her, would copy her Mardi Gras ball dress from
the Dresden china shepherdess in the parlor. The grandfather, returned from the grave for this story, orders Amy to make her costume
more respectable, but Amy argues that he had been looking at the
Dresden shepherdess for years without objection. To Mr. Rhea,
however, art and life are different. Amy obeys but appears at the
party dressed even more daringly.

Gabriel, Harry, and Mariana, Harry's fiancé (and perhaps a romantic rendering of Harrison Porter's wife, Mary Alice), all watch
Amy's behavior with some dismay as young men, some of rather
dubious character, flock about her. Later that night a former suitor
named Raymond and dressed as Jean Lafitte arrives, goes onto the
gallery with Amy, and according to family legend may have kissed
her, whereupon Gabriel challenges the pirate to a duel and Harry
defends Amy's honor by shooting at Raymond. The legend goes on
and on with the events taking on the overtones of a romantic Southern novel: Harry's flight to Mexico, Amy's dramatic ride with him
to the border, Gabriel sent away and disinherited, the wedding of

Gabriel and Amy, their honeymoon in New Orleans, and finally Amy's death six weeks after the wedding.

These stock scenes, presented to the children as reality, are challenged in parts II and III. Part II, set in 1904 after the death of the grandmother and after the children have been sent to a convent school, begins by contrasting the sedate, dull convent lives the girls live with the anti-Catholic stories the girls have read about nuns immured in convents and killing their babies. The girls have to give up trying to fit those violent stories to their life. They are indeed "immured" in the convent, but not in the sense meant in the trashy novels they read in the summer. Being "immured" gives a feeling of glamor to their dull, sterile lives. They are "hedged and confined," isolated in their muslin-curtained cells at night (just as Stephen is confined in *A Portrait of the Artist as a Young Man*), cut off from the outside world except on Saturday afternoons when they are allowed, if they have not broken too many regulations, to attend the races.

They meet Gabriel on one of those Saturdays, and Miranda begins to have doubts about the mythic figure she had long heard of. He is not the romantic hero of family legend; he is a fat, red-faced man whom Miranda recognizes immediately as a drunkard. He is still infatuated with the myth of Amy, a myth that has ruined him. His horse Miss Lucy wins the race that day, at a hundred-to-one odds, but the children see the horse as a trembling wild-eyed creature with a nosebleed, a reality far removed from Miranda's romantic view of racing. The scene is a counterpoint to Miranda's shedding her romantic picture of Gabriel.

The children are taken to a cheap hotel in Elysian Fields to see Miss Honey, Gabriel's second wife, who all her married life has been compared unfavorably with Amy. Miranda observes that Miss Honey, contrary to her name, is sharp and vinegary. The girls are dismayed at seeing the Gabriel myth destroyed, but they are not then able to conect their dismay with the Amy legend. Their great disappointment is in learning that the money they had won at the races is to go into the bank, where it is, as far as they are concerned, lost.

In "Part III: (1912)," after her confrontation with Cousin Eva, who like Eve, brings knowledge, Miranda reevaluates the family legends and vows not to be bound by the myths of the older generations. Now eighteen, she is returning to Texas to attend the funeral of Gabriel, who was faithful to Amy to the last and chose to be buried by her instead of Miss Honey.

In the sleeping car on the train, Miranda sits with Cousin Eva who tells her own story about Amy. Suffering from ugliness and from being the daughter of a beautiful woman, Eva did not share the romantic view of Amy and never regarded her as a ravishing beauty. She hints at the scandal surrounding Amy and speaks openly of Gabriel's unhappiness during the honeymoon. Tuberculosis, she says, is not romantic; Amy was driven to her illness by the feverish sexual rivalries of the late Victorian times, Eva insists. When Miranda repeats the family version of events, Eva calls her a "poor baby" and "innocent" and announces that knowledge would not hurt, that Miranda should not continue in a romantic haze. Eva, an amazingly complex character, perhaps speaks more of the truth than the family had; but, more important, she brings enlightenment.

In parts 1 and 2, Miranda seldom speaks to anyone; Miranda's sister is in many scenes, but the two sisters seem almost entirely separated; the scenes describing life in the convent, and with Miss Honey and Gabriel in Elysian Fields, emphasize the feeling of isolation; and Eva, breaking the fiction of the past, forces Miranda even further apart from the family and the past. Miranda then can ask herself where are her time and her place, but she has no ready answer. Secretly, she imagines that she can free herself from the family and the past, that she will not even remember them. She rejects the stories of the past and the relatives gathered for Gabriel's funeral, whose life, Harry says without irony, "was just one perpetual picnic." Miranda knows that she cannot go back to her husband and his family; family ties, she thinks, inundate her with love and hatred. She is, at this point, Prospero's daughter intent upon making her own discoveries.

As is true of many of Porter's stories, "Old Mortality" ends in isolation and desolation: it concludes with a statement bringing together the incidents and making clear the symbols of isolation. Miranda tries to fathom the meaning of the past and her own way of looking at it. Her final thoughts are, however, heavily weighted with irony: "I don't want any promises, I won't have false hopes, I won't be romantic about myself. I can't live in their world any longer, she told herself, listening to the voices back of her. Let them tell their stories to each other. Let them go on explaining how things happened. I don't care. At least I can know the truth about what happens to me, she assured herself silently, making a promise to herself, in her hopefulness, her ignorance."

The myth of the South, a hint at another reality, self-knowledge, and self-deception are among the important themes of the story. If *the* truth about events and people is not revealed, at least some of it is, and "the ruines of forgotten times" have been exposed.

Miranda the Woman

"Pale Horse, Pale Rider."

And I looked, and behold a pale horse: and his name that sat on him was Death, and Hell followed with him. And power was given unto them over the fourth part of the earth, to kill with sword, and with hunger, and with death, and with the beasts of the earth. (Rev. 6:8)

When "Pale Horse, Pale Rider"[13] (1938) was being adapted for a television play, Porter told an interviewer:

"I was quite young during World War in Denver and I had a job on *Rocky Mountain News*. Bill the city editor [the city editor of her story is named Bill], put me to covering the theaters.

"I met a boy, an army lieutenant. . . . Our time was so short and we were much in love. But we were shy. It was a step forward and two steps back with us. . . . I was taken ill with the flu. They gave me up. The paper had my obit set in type. I've seen the correspondence between my father and sister on plans for my funeral . . . I knew I was dying. I felt a strange state of—what is it the Greeks called it?—euphoria. . . . But I didn't die. I mustered the will to live."

"And the boy, Miss Porter?"

"It's in the story. . . . He died. . . . It's a true story. . . . It seems to me true that I died then, I died once, and I have never feared death since."[14]

Porter earlier told Robert Van Gelder, in an interview published in *Writers and Writing* in 1946, much the same story: that she had influenza during the epidemic and was near death. She believed, Van Gelder reported in the interview, "that it is true that the moment of death holds something like revelation." The novel was Porter's attempt "to record that experience," and it was "the best story she has yet written." Porter told several variations of this story. During the last years of her life she insisted that the character Adam's name was Alexander Barclay, who translated *Das Narrenschiff* into English. [15]

The opening scene, a dream sequence, states the story's important themes: rejection yet love of the past, and knowledge yet rejection of death. In her early morning dream, Miranda rejects Fiddler, her grandmother's horse, and Miss Lucy, Amy's horse, for Graylie. Gray, the color of her chosen horse, indicates her own ambivalent feelings, although her reason for choosing Graylie demonstrates her wish to win the race with death and the devil. "I'll take Graylie because he is not afraid of bridges," she thinks in her dream, and it is obvious that she has in mind the folk belief that the evil spirits dare not, as Burns's Tam O'Shanter and Irving's Ichabod Crane knew, cross a running stream. The green stranger was well known in the Rhea household, and had "been welcomed by" the grandfather and by a distantly removed aunt, a young kitten, and an old hound. In not mentioning the grandmother, does Miranda, even in her dream, preserve Sophia Jane from death or does she imply that Sophia Jane did not welcome the stranger? There had been too much "storied dust" in the household, too much ancestor worship, too many conventions and deceptions, and yet the past is all she has. The stranger rides beside her easily, but Miranda shouts that she would not go with him "this time," fully aware that there would be another time.

Awake, Miranda's non–dream world is just as nightmarish as her dream world. World War I is on, with its pestilence and death; influenza is sweeping the country; professional patriots are attempting to force Miranda to spend money she does not have for Liberty Bonds; at the theater she is forced to hear an emotional, dishonest speech by a bond salesman. Added to this is the limbo of her work, which stretches from afternoon until late at night—a round of reviewing plays and vaudeville acts, of having to face the seedy has-beens she pans, of working on a newspaper that prints war rumors and propaganda and with a tubercular sports writer constantly explaining why he is not at war and a city editor who is a parody of city editors. Behind all this looms the war itself. The key to many scenes is found in Miranda's thoughts at the theater: "We dare not say a word to each other of our desperation, we are speechless animals letting ourselves be destroyed, and why? Does anybody here believe the things we say to each other?"

Miranda finds some stability and peace with Adam Barclay, the young Texas-born officer who comes by accident to the same rooming house where she lives. The descriptions of him, on a realistic level, emphasize his handsomeness and his masculinity; but, on a mythic level, he represents Adam, the first man, made from a bar of clay; Isaac, subject to sacrificial slaughter; and Adonis, the handsome god. Adam, masculinity personified, is completely removed from Miranda's world of poetry and the imagination, and it is Miranda who is able to intuit and prophesy his death. When she sees his face in a bad light, she has a glimpse of an older Adam: "the face of the man he would not live to be."

Miranda cannot voice her premonitions, cannot tell Adam, as they dance in the tawdry hall, of her pain or of the searing question "why can we not save each other?" Nor can she tell him of the dumb show she sees behind him—the young couple in the corner, who, after tears and kisses, settle whatever problem they have and sit looking at each other "into the hell they shared." Contrasted with the dumb show and Miranda's interpretation of it is the conversation she hears at the next table: a young girl telling her date how a young man gauchely tried to seduce her by getting her drunk. The grossness of the seducer and the narrator contrasted with the incident Miranda observes but does not hear is a brilliant scene of appearance-reality, an ever-present theme in the work.

From the first dream at the beginning of the story, Miranda is infected with fever from the influenza epidemic then sweeping the country. With the illness ravaging her mind and body, the feverish atmosphere becomes more intense, and she has fewer and fewer lucid moments. Adam comes to look after her, but she talks, then drifts off, transported into the perpetual snow of the mountains, chilled to the bone by cold. Seeking warmth, in her dreams she enters into tropical scenes combining her early memories of the grandmother's farm—including the hovering buzzard, described in "Noon Wine: The Sources"—before sailing from this unreal but known world to a jungle. She sets sail on a river, a combination of all the rivers she has known and, symbolically, the river Styx. The jungle is a place of death, filled with animals, bathed in a sulphur-colored light, with rotting trees in the slime. Waving to herself in bed—saying good-bye to her physical body—she sails into the jungle, with voices crying out danger and war.

Not wanted by the Sisters in the Catholic hospital, or by Mrs. Hobbe, owner of the rooming house, Miranda, thus doubly rejected, tries to talk to Adam about her life, often drifting into the past tense. She does not speak of her grandmother or her first husband; she does not know whether she had been happy; she has lived and hoped, but was always preparing for a future. Only when she talks of the joys of colors and sounds does she feel strongly about living, and only then can she use the present tense.

Afraid to go to sleep, Miranda wants to sing the old Negro spiritual she had heard sung in the cotton fields. She and Adam sing, "Pale horse, pale rider, done taken my lover away," a thematic restatement from the first dream. Miranda knows that in the song all were taken away by death except the singer, who is left to mourn. Both Adam and Miranda are singing, and they cannot know which will be spared.

After the two confess their love for each other, Miranda again drifts into a dream in which arrows keep striking Adam, who falls, then rises, to be struck again. Miranda, attempting to shield Adam from perpetual death and resurrection, is struck through the heart— with Cupid's arrow—but Adam falls dead.

Finally taken to a hospital in a highly feverish state, Miranda would not believe that Adam had come to see her; and, in another dream, she sees Dr. Hildesheim as a poisoner and murderer, though he is attempting to save her life. Ironically, Miranda subconsciously believes the anti-German propaganda she can reject when conscious. She tries to explain to the doctor that she is not afraid of him, but she is swept into unconsciousness again. Wandering in her dream toward oblivion, she finds herself without feeling, without attributes. Literally and symbolically, she is at the point of death.

In *Images of Truth,* Glenway Wescott notes that the vision of heaven that follows gave Porter much trouble. "She told me," Wescott writes, "that she herself, at the end of World War I, had experienced this part of what she had created this heroine to experience and to make manifest; and because, no doubt, it really was heaven, she found herself unable to re-see it with her lively, healthy eyes." Wescott urged her not to try, since heaven is indescribable; but Porter did make the attempt and did succeed. In her mystical vision, Miranda finds quiet instead of the noise of the jungle, serenity instead of violence, purity instead of corruption, understanding instead of separation. She finds a soft green meadow, much the same as that in Blake's "The Chimney Sweeper" in *Songs of Innocence.*

Miranda is, however, repulsed by the colorless sunlight; she will not accept life under the rainbow, God's gift to Noah.

She becomes conscious again on Armistice Day and hears old crones singing patriotic songs. She does not know how she will be able to bear the drabness of the world after the reality of her mystical dream; for in the real world she now feels only grayness, and she is acutely aware of her alienation. She does not mean to live in the world and yet cannot will her death. Nothing she would ever see would rival "a child's dream of the heavenly meadow."

Society conspires to bring her to health again; her acquaintances come, and she is able to make idle conversation, to go through the formal rhetoric of a sick visit. The friends bring her mail, which she puts aside for a few days. Forced by the nurse to read the letters, Miranda learns of Adam's death and knows that she gave him the illness that killed him, knows that she had returned from death because she wanted to be with him, but that he was at that moment already dead.

Next, Miranda makes her symbolic preparations for entering the world of withered beings who believe they are alive: cosmetics for her mask, gray gauntlets for protection, gray hose without embroidery, and a walking stick. The color gray is consistent with her feeling about the world she is about to enter and is thematically connected with the gray horse of the first dream; it is also a rejection of the mourning clothes her grandmother habitually wore. Sarah Youngblood in "Structure and Imagery in Katherine Anne Porter's 'Pale Horse, Pale Rider,' " concluded her study of the story: "Her mental image of herself as Lazarus come forth with 'top hat and stick' is a dual vision of herself as he has been and as she will be in the world where appearances must be maintained." Left to mourn the lover taken away by the pale rider, Miranda at first tries but fails to call into her presence the ghost of Adam. Her conscious fears are put aside as she accepts a world without war, houses without noise, streets without people, and "the dead cold light of tomorrow." She knows, as one initiated into both heaven and hell, life and death, "Now there would be time for everything."

Born into a world seemingly stable but in decay, disorder and disruption, Miranda lives at first under the protection of the grandmother who by force of will tries but never succeeds in bringing order to the world of the home and to the larger world of the family farm. Curious to know but generally not comprehending the full nature of her discoveries, Miranda learns of the glories of the South and the traditions of chivalry, but she also hears of the misery of the Negro; she sees her grandmother's constant companion, the former slave Nannie, move away from the demanding Rheas after the death of Sophia Jane; she learns of the social order of rural Texas and of the mysteries of the womb and tomb; she is afraid of the weeping sound that was connected in her mind with death but she accepts a scientific explanation; she dreams of being beautiful, of reliving the aristocratic past of the family but finds that she cannot accept the myth of the past as told by her family; she elopes from a confining convent but has to leave her husband in order to find her own truths; at the age of twenty-four she lives in an utterly chaotic world at war but finds in the midst of death that death can no longer frighten her; seeing herself as the agent of death for her lover, to whom she had returned from near death, she covers her sadness with a despair beyond weeping. When we see an older Miranda, a Miranda who has gone gladly into this brave new world, she stands in a tropical market of a strange city, surrounded by bustling life and physical decay, confronted by an Indian vendor selling sickly sweet candied baby animals, and she sees at that moment a vision of her initiation into some of the mysteries of the world. Heaven and hell, love and sex, love and hate, truth and mendacity, life and death, order and disorder—all these Miranda experiences in Porter's exploration of her own mythic reality in the Miranda stories.

Chapter Four

To Tell a Straight Story

The stories that follow are divided into four thematic groupings. The first four stories have a southern or southwestern setting and some have recognizable autobiographical details. "He" and "Noon Wine" are set against the familiar southern background but are concerned with poor whites instead of the aristocratic Rheas. "The Jilting of Granny Weatherall" seems to be a fictional version of the death of Catherine Anne Porter, but the portrayal is quite different from that of Grandmother Rhea in the Miranda stories. "Magic" is a brilliant Jamesian experiment in point of view.

In the next three stories Porter deftly explores three themes in the universal human condition. "Rope" is a universalized rendering of the battle of the sexes; "The Downward Path to Wisdom," one of her most stylistically dazzling stories, is a still fresh insight into the child-to-adult journey; and "Theft," perhaps a perfect story, unmercifully lays bare the conflict between myth and reality.

The following two stories, "The Cracked Looking-Glass" and "A Day's Work," deal with Irish immigrants in the United states. These stories are, as Marjorie Ryan points out in "*Dubliners* and the Stories of Katherine Anne Porter," "Joycean in techniques as well as in theme." Ryan notes that the stories are an "objective rendering of the situation," that the author does not comment, and that, in general, "the meaning is implicit in the action."

The last two stories concern Germany and Germans. In "Holiday" the reader sees German immigrants in Texas, as they are viewed by a deeply troubled young woman who resembles Miranda. The last story, "The Leaning Tower," was written while *Ship of Fools* was still in embryonic form, but the time is Germany of 1931, when Porter was living there. We see Berlin and the Berliners through the consciousness of Charles Upton, a sensitive observer struggling to understand the reality behind what he sees.

Southern, Southwestern, and Autobiographical Stories

"He."   In "He" (1927) Porter uses as background the poverty of her childhood in the small town of Kyle, Texas, to deal with a hopelessly deformed or mentally incompetent person and his place in society and the family, a theme she later explored in "Holiday" and in the character of Herr Glocken in *Ship of Fools*.[1] "He" is told with both objectivity and irony, and its ending shows compassion for both mother and child.

The Whipples are a Southern family not willing to admit that they are "poor whites." They rather resemble Porter's own family and the fictional Thompsons in "Noon Wine." Mr. Whipple is a realist, ready to talk to neighbors about their hard life, but his wife insists on pretending to a life of gentility and prosperity—just as she pretends love for their simpleminded son. She announces her love for Him ("He" is never referred to by any other name and is always capitalized) to everyone she sees, but her professed love is a cover for hatred. She allows Him to climb trees, to do more work than He should, to handle the bees because He seems not to notice the stings, to lead a dangerous bull, to steal a pig from its ferocious mother. Covered with fat, He is more harmless beast than human; the pink pig killed for Sunday dinner is described in almost the same terms as those used for Him.

Adna and Emly (as with Hinry in the Miranda stories, these spellings approximate the regional pronunciation), Mr. Whipple, and the neighbors are minor but necessary figures who make significant contributions to the theme of the story. Mrs. Whipple is proud that her two normal children are fed and dressed properly, that they are able to leave the "hard times" on the farm. She worries about what the neighbors will think if she allows Him to become ill or injured, but the neighbors speculate on the bad blood that has produced such a child.

One winter near Christmas (the unwary are warned not to fall into the trap of identifying Him with Jesus), He falls on the ice, and thrashes about in a fit. Some years before, when He had had a serious illness, the Whipples had waited two days before going for the doctor; but this time His suffering is more obvious, and though they go for help immediately, it is clear that even the doctor cannot help. The Whipples keep Him at home for a time, but the doctor finally told them they must take Him to the county home. Mr. Whipple, oppressed by his poverty, is relieved, but Mrs. Whipple is concerned only that the neighbors will look down on them for turning to charity.

On the way to the home, He begins to cry, and Mrs. Whipple imagines that He is remembering all the mistreatment and hardships of His life. She cries too, and for the first time the reader has compassion for this vain, often cruel mother: "she had loved Him as much as she possibly could, there were Adna and Emly who had to be thought of too, there was nothing she could do to make up to Him for His life."

As hypocritical as she had been, she had instinctively fought for her normal children, thinly covering her hatred for Him with Christian piety. But her last thoughts strip the false morality away: "Oh, what a mortal pity He was ever born." He was beyond help, He could receive but could not return love. The Whipples are too human and too poor to be able to do more than they did for Him. The Müllers in "Holiday" are never shown identifying with Ottilie, for they had forgotten their kinship with her. They are, however, less outwardly cruel to her than the Whipples are to their son.

"He" is a particularly bleak story, for the corrosive effects of poverty and of a mentally defective child, combined with the bleakness of the seasons—many of the scenes are set in fall or winter—and the relentless focusing of the reader's attention on the hopeless creature "He," are all woven into a compellingly pessimistic study.

"Noon Wine."   The setting for "Noon Wine" (1936) is a small south Texas farm from 1896 to 1905, roughly the same time that Porter lived in that region.[2] In fact, as Givner has convincingly shown, the Thompsons were actually relatives of the Porter family, and Porter spent time on their farm. The story retains the family name, the family personality traits, and the name of the hired man, Helton. But in her essay about the story, Porter does not admit that she was a part of this poverty-stricken family.

The story opens with a stranger's appearance at the farm of Royal Earle Thompson, a proud man engaged in the disagreeable, feminine task of churning. The stranger, seeking work, is hired, and for the next few years Olaf Helton, a reticent man who plays the same tune over and over on his harmonica, helps make the farm prosper.

Nine years after Helton arrives, another stranger comes, a Homer T. Hatch, looking for Mr. Helton. While Thompson is talking to

Hatch, they can hear Helton playing the harmonica, playing the tune Hatch identifies as a "Scandahoovian song." "It says," he reports, "something about starting out in the morning feeling so good you can't hardly stand it, so you drink up all your likker before noon. All the likker, y'understand, that you was saving for the noon lay-off." Hatch has come to return Helton to the asylum, to which he had been committed after killing his brother in a fight over a harmonica.

Perhaps thinking that Hatch is going to injure Helton, Thompson kills Hatch and, though exonerated in a trial, he, like the Ancient Mariner, keeps trying to explain to his neighbors just what had happened. One night after an all-day trip to explain the killing, Mr. Thompson has a nightmare, and Mrs. Thompson cries out, "Oh, oh, don't! Don't! Don't!" Mr. Thompson cries, "Light the lamp," and the two sons rush into the room, believing that Mr. Thompson (once a murderer always a murderer) has attempted to harm their mother. "You touch her again and I'll blow your heart out!" one son says. Mr. Thompson, at this moment, feels utter defeat; he knew his neighbors did not believe his story; now he sees his own sons do not believe him. He says he is going for the doctor, but instead takes his gun, goes into the field, and writes: "Before Almighty God, the great judge of all before who I am about to appear, I do hereby solemnly swear that I did not take the life of Mr. Homer T. Hatch on purpose. It was done in defense of Mr. Helton. . . . I have told all this to the judge and the jury and they let me off but nobody believes it. This is the only way I can prove I am not a cold blooded murderer like everybody seems to think." Then he shoots himself.

In " 'Noon Wine': The Sources" Porter continued the mythology that she was a southern aristocrat recalling the grim story of the plain people of her section of Texas. In her account, she attempted to show how an artist lives a story three times: "first in the series of actual events that, directly or indirectly, have combined to set up that commotion in his mind and senses that causes him to write the story; second, in memory; and third, in recreation of this chaotic stuff."

She remembers when she was a child hearing one late summer afternoon, when "the sky was a clear green-blue with long streaks of burning rose in it" and filled with swooping bats, the sound of a thundering shotgun, and a long-drawn-out scream. "How did I know it was death?" she asks, and replies, "We are born knowing death." Later she remembers watching the hearse go by and members of her family saying: "Poor Pink Hodges—old man A—got him just like he said he would."

When she was about nine, she noticed a strange horse and buggy in the drive and saw a man and woman inside the house, talking to her grandmother, the woman "in a faded cotton print dress and a wretched little straw hat," a woman with the marks of "life-starvation" all over her. She kept her eyes on her twisting hands as her husband in a coarse voice said, "I swear, it was in self-defense! . . . If you don't believe me, ask my wife here. She saw it. My wife won't lie!" And the wife answered each time, "Yes, that's right. I saw it." Though Porter never knew the facts of the killing or the outcome, she knew that the woman was made to lie; that she did it unwillingly; but that her husband, dishonest as he was, made her lie in an attempt to make his lie true. This man, unlike the "foolishly proud" man in the story, was "a great loose-faced, blabbing man full of guilt and fear."

Not long afterwards, Porter was with her father when they saw a "tall, black-whiskered man on horseback, sitting so straight his chin was level with his Adam's apple," with a flamboyant black "hat on the side of his head." Her father said, "That's Ralph Thomas, the proudest man in seven counties." She asked what he was proud of, and her father replied, "I suppose the horse. It's a very fine horse." She saw then that the man was ridiculous yet pathetic. (This story about Ralph Thomas may have been introduced as protection, for after "Noon Wine" was published, as Givner points out in *Katherine Anne Porter, A Life,* the Thompsons and the Skaggses saw themselves portrayed as "ignorant, dangerous people," and they thought Porter "should be sued.")

On another trip Porter says she saw "a bony, awkward, tired-looking man, tilted in a kitchen chair against the wall of his comfortless shack . . . a thatch of bleached-looking hair between his eyebrows, blowing away at a doleful tune on his harmonica . . . the very living image of loneliness. I was struck with pity for this stranger, his eyes closed against the alien scene, consoling himself with such poor music." Later, she says, she learned he was a Swedish farm worker. The recollection totally ignores the fact that she actually lived on the Thompson farm where Helton was the hired man and whose background must have been known to her.

Porter explains the process of memory and artistic creativity she used in the story:

I saw . . . a few mere flashes of a glimpse here and there, one time or another; but I do know why I remembered them, and why in my memory they slowly took on their separate lives in a story. It is because there radiated from each one of those glimpses of strangers some element, some quality that arrested my attention at a vital moment of my own growth, and caused me, a child, to stop short and look outward, away from myself; to look at another human being with that attention and wonder and speculation which ordinarily, and very naturally, I think, a child lavishes only on himself.

In "Noon Wine" Pink Hodges is merged with the Swedish farm worker, who becomes the "eternal Victim"; the whining man, the killer, is merged with the proudest man in seven counties; the killer's wife, a pathetic figure, becomes the genteel Mrs. Thompson.

In Porter's short novel, Mr. Thompson—one of the common people, but with the pretentious name Royal Earle—has married slightly above himself. Mrs. Thompson, in her gentility and ill health, is typical of her time—she is bound by a moral code dictated by a frontier religion that she finds immutable. Mr. Thompson sees himself as a murderer and makes his wife lie, hoping the lie will alter the fact; but she too thinks of him as a murderer—she cannot lie to herself. By forcing her to consent to lie, he has murdered her spirit; but she can never do more than publicly lie—she can never help him redeem himself by telling the final lie, by insisting that she really did see, that he did kill in self-defense.

Thompson's motives are mixed; Helton brought a better life to the Thompsons; Thompson did not want his new prosperity damaged. Hatch was obviously an evil man, and society agrees that Thompson should not be punished. The courts do not convict him, but he is still a murderer. Helton is a man beyond good and evil, a murderer himself, his own victim and the victim of others.

"Noon Wine" is concerned with one of the central problems in Porter's fiction: the efforts of people to cope with evil. None of the Thompsons is fully capable of understanding or opposing the evil of Hatch and the evil legacy he left behind or the mixed good and evil character of Helton. Mr. Thompson never understands his motives for killing Hatch and because he cannot understand he is driven to self-destruction. Mrs. Thompson cannot tell the ultimate lie that would save her husband. The Thompson boys believe the worst of their father. Helton has largely overcome his psychic malaise, and perhaps his compulsion to do violence; but he lives in a private hell that no one understands. Hatch's motivations cannot be explained away in terms of financial rewards; he is the evil principle, beyond understanding. "There is nothing," Porter says, "in any of these beings tough enough to work the miracle of redemption in them."

"The Jilting of Granny Weatherall." "The Jilting of Granny Weatherall" (1929) may be seen as another of Porter's creative uses of her "usable" past; it is a somewhat more objective, even more fictional, presentation of the actual grandmother.[3] Or, one may see the story as an extension of Porter's use of "historic memory," as Ray B. West has called it, and see that the death "reflects a particular, but common, attitude toward death." John Hagopian has found the moral of the story "to be that the universe has no order, the proper bridegroom never comes—to expect him will inevitably lead to cruel disillusionment." More recently, Darlene Unrue argues that Granny "has identified the absent George with Christ and feels abandoned by both."[4]

The story is presented by an omniscient observer who reports the dying Ellen Weatherall's stream-of-consciousness review of her life. During the last day of her life, old Granny Weatherall, almost eighty, moves back and forth from consciousness to unconsciousness, from the present to the past, conjuring up all her old fears and dreams. Like Porter's fictional Grandmother Rhea, Granny Weatherall has been a strong-willed, active woman who buried a young husband and reared a large family. For sixty years she has been trying to forget that on the day of her first proposed marriage, her fiancé, George, had jilted her. She later married John and bore his children, naming the first George and the last, which she wished had been George's, Hapsy—quite probably a diminutive of Happiness.

On the morning of her last day, she is still a cantankerous old woman. She can still focus her eyes, can still hear and is annoyed by the whisperings of young Dr. Harry, on a house call, and her daughter Cornelia. Things do seem to float, however, and the whisperings sometimes take on strange sounds, as if they were the leaves blowing outside. Back and forth in time she goes, thinking of her orderly house, the clock with the lion on it gathering dust (a reference to James's "Beast in the Jungle"), representing the disorder that she, like Sophia Jane, has constantly to fight. She plagues dutiful Cornelia with whom she lives, but it is Hapsy, the daughter now dead, whom she really wants with her. She wants to see her first fiancé, to tell him about her husband and her children: "Tell him I was given back everything he took away and more. Oh, no, oh, God, no, there was something else besides the house and the man and the children. Oh, surely they were not all? What was it? Something not given back."

Her thoughts about her loss are similar to the exploration of loss in James's short story, "The Beast in the Jungle"; and even her name suggests Weatherend, the name of the house where the James story begins. Some of the descriptions are similar: James wrote of May Bartram's household, "The perfection of household care, of high polish and finish, always reigned in her rooms, but they now looked most as if everything had been wound up, tucked in, put away." Porter wrote, "Things were finished somehow when the time came; thank God there was always a little margin over for peace: then a person could spread out the plan of life and tuck in the edges orderly. It was good to have everything clean and folded away."

Granny tries to delude herself into believing that there is nothing wrong with her, just as she had deluded herself that she could forget her jilting. When Hapsy appears to her in her delusion, Granny seems to be herself and "to be Hapsy also, and the baby on Hapsy's arm was Hapsy and himself and herself, all at once." Himself is undoubtedly George, whom she cannot call by name. Hapsy says, "I thought you'd never come," and they start to kiss, but Granny, then near death, is called back when Cornelia speaks.

By nighttime she is barely able to speak or focus her eyes, and she does not understand what Father Connolly is doing as he administers the last rites of the Catholic church: she has a rosary in her hand "and Father Connolly murmured Latin in a very solemn voice and tickled her feet. My God, will you stop that nonsense?" Only when she drops the rosary and takes instead the thumb of her son Jimmy does she realize that her living children have come for her death. In a panic, she begins to think of all the unfinished things she wanted done. She asks God for a sign, but there is none. Again there is a priest in the house but no bridegroom—in this second jilting, the absent bridegroom is Jesus of Matthew 25:1–13—and she cannot forgive being jilted again; she would not be jilted again: "She stretched herself with a deep breath and blew out the light."

The death scene has many similarities with Miranda's near death in "Pale Horse, Pale Rider," for both emphasize the darkness, the pale light, the grayness. Gray is the color of the fog and smoke that crept over the bright field where everything is planted orderly, and it is the color of George, for "the thought of him was a smoky cloud from hell"; one is reminded of the "grey impalpable world" at the conclusion of Joyce's "The Dead." As in "Pale Horse, Pale Rider," the grays of death and the green of life are constantly juxtaposed, just as the images of light, the lamp, candles, matches, flame, are contrasted with those of dark, of fear, of betrayal and death. Smoke and fog hide approaching death, as orchards, fields, rows of crops and fruit trees, green rugs, and polished floors represent happiness and the joy of life. Granny Weatherall's mind drifts with all these images, just as Molly Bloom's thoughts drift in the last section of *Ulysses*; Molly answers yes, but Granny, willful to the end, denies death its triumph—she blows out her own light.

As in other Porter stories, the truth here is bitter and grimly determined. The ending, an echo of James again, is fully as inevitable as is the end for John Marcher, who though he saw the lurking beast rise, leap, and miss, could avoid it only when he "flung himself, face down, on the tomb." Porter learned her lessons from James well. Her story has all the finesse, skill, and symbolism of the master himself; but, although there are Jamesian echoes, the story is uniquely her own.

"**Magic**."   Based on a story Porter had heard told by a black maid in New Orleans, "Magic" (1928) is another example of Porter's use of Jamesian narrative technique.[5] Its form is a dramatic monologue by a Negro maid who was once a servant in a bordello but is now employed in the home of Madame Blanchard. The maid prides herself on her French blood and good character, but she works where work is to be found. Her story about a bit of magic at the house of prostitution where she once worked is told to amuse Madame Blanchard, whose hair she is brushing. She sees a receptive audience for her tale of magic when Madame Blanchard remarks to the laundress that the sheets wear out so quickly they must be bewitched. Acutely aware of her role as an entertainer, the maid emphasizes the scenes of violence, the peculiar monetary system

used by the madam, and the exact details of the making of a voodoo
charm to bring back Ninette, a run-away prostitute. The maid had,
she insists, seen too many things, terrible events that she willingly
and frivolously tells her new mistress. Madame Blanchard is another
of Porter's fictional characters who are based on real persons. As
Givner points out, in the 1920s Porter lived for a time in the
rooming house of Madame Katrina Blanchard in Greenwich Village.[6]

The fictional Madame Blanchard sits at her dressing table, apparently a little bored, as the maid begins her story, saying perhaps
maliciously that she hopes the violent, perverse tale she is going to
tell will rest her mistress. Madame Blanchard does not object to
hearing the story; in fact, at two different times she asks the maid
to go on with it. The first interruption is of special interest: Madame
Blanchard complains that her hair is being pulled at the time when
the maid is explaining her former madam's special understanding
with the police, who allowed the girls to stay with her unless they
were sick (a euphemism for venereal disease). While it may be true
that the maid does pull the hair, it is just as likely that the mistress,
distressed by the implications of the story and its undermining of
the institutions of middle- and upper-class life, may have complained
about the hair pulling as a nervous protest. Madame Blanchard,
showing no compassion for the prostitutes, is cold and expression-
less, qualities she holds in common with the madam.

The maid and Madame Blanchard provide the frame for the story
of life in the brothel, which was, perhaps, not much different from
any other way of life. The household is controlled by the madam
who, with no human emotion, constantly cheats the girls, argues
over money, fights by unfair means. When Ninette, the most called-
for girl, announces, independently, that she is leaving, the madam
beats her furiously and kicks her in the groin before turning her
out into the street. Ninette is engaged in a profession that is, as
the narrator sees it, just a business. In defying the madam, who
has the support of the police and pimps, Ninette, an outcast of
society, is courageous, but her revolt is doomed from the first.

The Negro cook, a woman with much French blood also, but
with a bad character the narrator insists, makes a magic brew to
bring Ninette back. After the maid finishes with the lurid details
of the making of the magic brew, Madame Blanchard interrupts
again—thus returning the reader to the frame—closes her perfume

bottle, and asks, "Yes, and then?" Yes, the maid says, the charm worked: Ninette returned and was ordered upstairs to dress for work.

The narrator's account of the events, toned down in language but with certain of the violent scenes emphasized, is not to be considered the truth, but a dramatic version of it. The narrator, for instance, is never aware of the ironies involved: she refers to the bordello as a fancy house; she believes that the magic potion had brought Ninette back; she misses the significance of the man's greeting "Welcome home" to Ninette on her return. The story ends on a final note of irony: Ninette, who dared to revolt, to flee the corruption of the sordid house, finds no haven in a world itself corrupt and sordid, and she returns to the madam, where she would again be cheated, but where she is in demand by her customers. The maid ends the story as if it were a fairy tale and everyone lived happily ever after: "And after that she lived there quietly."

Joan Givner notes that the story "is a first version of the theme, the passive promotion of evil by innocent people, which would run through [Porter's] works in a steady, unbroken line until it reached its fullest expression in *Ship of Fools*."[7] Helen L. Leath has argued that readers should pay attention to the story's form and to the storyteller. Leath thinks that the observant maid, a believer in magic, "is offering her services as spellcaster to Madame Blanchard." She sees the story as "a struggle for supremacy between two female characters." She argues that the maid is not telling an entertaining story but is attempting to gain a commanding place in the household through magic.[8]

Whatever Porter's intentions, and however one wishes to read it, this story of five pages is one of great complexity, uniting several creative techniques: Jamesian point-of-view; the frame with its characterizations of the maid and the mistress; the interplay between the madam, the maid, and Ninette; the subtle psychological probings; and the bitter social criticism. A major achievement, this story is too little appreciated.

Stories with Universal Themes

"Rope." Porter's failed marriage in 1926 to Ernest Stock provided the material for "Rope" (1928).[9] The "he" and "she" of the story, never identified by name, are tied together in marriage; but, in their love-hate relationship, they are hanging each other, giving one another enough rope, forcing the other on the ropes, and both are at the end of their ropes. The story is another of Porter's examinations of marriage, love, hate, and frustration. Unlike her other stories dealing with marriage—such as "That Tree" or "The Cracked Looking-Glass"—the exact time, place, and setting and the background of the characters are not given. By implication we know it is late fall, that the setting is in the country, and that both he and she earn money, his income being larger.

The first and last paragraphs emphasize the tranquility of the rural scene. They have only been in the country three days, and already they see each other as hayseedish characters. This deceptively peaceful scene is soon replaced with corrosive argument. Ostensibly, she begins the quarrel because he forgets to buy coffee. Instead he had impulsively bought a rope, for which he could think of no real use.

The indirect quotations emphasize the bitterness of the quarrel. The rope has broken the eggs; she has no ice to keep them until the next day; she would not have the rope in her pantry. He does not know what ties them together, why he should not just clear out. She is too busy organizing the house to enjoy the country; he does not think the house should ride them. He returns to the store, two miles away, for her coffee, for her laxative, and for the other items she suddenly remembered. He takes the rope to exchange it, but secretly hides it behind a rock.

When he appears again, rope in hand, masculine pride still intact, she is waiting serenely for him, supper ready, unconcerned that he has "forgotten" to exchange the rope. She is playful, kittenish, talking baby talk. They hear a whippoorwill in a crab-apple tree— fittingly a tree with sour fruit—"calling all by himself. Maybe his girl stood him up. Maybe she did. She hoped to hear him once more, she loved whippoorwills. . . . He knew how she was, didn't he?" She projects her own feelings into the sad song of the bird, imagining that his mate has jilted him, wanting to hear the bird's song again.

The story ends on a note of tranquility masking the terrible battle that has just been fought. They have both said too much that cannot be forgotten, and many of the threads of the rope holding them together have been unraveled. The final line indicates that the husband is also aware of the implications of the quarrel and of her

interpretation of the bird's song: "Sure, he knew how she was."
The disastrous quarrel in "Rope" is similar to the corrosive Jenny-
David fights in *Ship of Fools*.

"The Downward Path to Wisdom." "The Downward Path
to Wisdom" (1939) was based on a childhood memory of Glenway
Wescott's, but it contains many veiled references to Porter's own
childhood, her ambivalent feelings about her grandmother, her belief that she had been rejected by her father and abandoned (through
death) by her mother.[10] It was written in the 1930s when Porter
and Wescott saw each other often. Givner pointedly notes that
Wescott "had been raised on a Wisconsin farm and his early life
had been soured by the hostility of a father who despised his effem-
inate, artistic son."[11]

The story's title is another of Porter's ironic contradictions: Stephen does not ascend to wisdom but travels downward in his journey
from innocence to experience, from blissful ignorance to knowledge,
from paradise to hell. An examination of the fiery furnace of childhood, the story concentrates on a few weeks in the life of a little
boy, who is most often called "baby" or "fellow" or "bad boy," and
who is not given his correct name, Stephen, until late in the story.
(Porter also used the name "Stephen" for her fictional grandfather,
thereby placing him with her other ineffectual men who are ma-
nipulated by dominant women.)

At the opening of the story, Stephen is a four-year-old child
described and treated as if he were an animal: when he is lifted into
his parents' bed, he sinks between them "like a bear cub in a warm
litter"; he crunches his peanuts "like a horse." His peanut eating
reminds one of the monkeys in "The Circus" and of Otto in "The
Leaning Tower" who is beaten as a child because his mother does
not like the sound of cracking walnuts. The story contains many
echoes of Joyce's *Portrait of the Artist as a Young Man* besides the
names of the central characters: Porter's Stephen calls a cat a meow,
and Joyce's Stephen Dedalus is told the story about a moocow;
Stephen is jeered at by the schoolchildren when he tries to make a
meow, and Stephen Dedalus is pushed into a square ditch; Stephen
eats peanuts and Stephen Dedalus is given a cachou.

Stephen is rejected in various ways. His mother does not like
peanut shells spilled all over her, and he is put out of bed and finally
out of the room while his parents quarrel over his eating the nuts.
Since the whole story is reported from Stephen's point of view, the

reader does not know exactly what goes on between the parents, only how it affects him. Rejected by both parents, he is soon rejected by the maid Marjory, who calls him a "dirty little old boy" because he does not want his breakfast; she even repeats what we learn later is the family opinion of Stephen's father—that he is mean. The fight between the parents becomes so intense that Stephen is sent suddenly to his grandmother's house to stay. He is frightened, even though he had been sent to her house before; he can think of only one comforting thing, his peanuts, and he cries for them.

Stephen's hostility toward the world is a natural reaction: he can never be certain of the reactions of those around him. His father gives the boy the peanuts and then scolds him for eating them. His Uncle David gives him balloons but turns on him when he takes others without permission. The old grandmother, seeing the hate building up over the boy, finally declares that she just wants to be left alone. The old servant Janet who takes him to school makes him feel guilty about sex.

All the adults had been expelled from paradise themselves, and the crucial scene in the story is Stephen's expulsion. At school, Stephen meets Frances, the archetypal Eve. To win her affection, he gives her balloons, but his offerings do not entice her. She is larger and more mature than he; when they dance at school, she wants to lead and humiliates him, saying he cannot dance. She also ridicules him to the other children, declaring that his artistic creation is a horse, not a cat. Stephen learns in his first days at school that popularity can be bought with favors but can vanish suddenly, leaving him a scapegoat, a figure of ridicule.

He and Frances sit together blowing up balloons, which swell, change colors, and become part of his dreams and aspirations; but they grow and grow, only to burst, a final disillusionment. "Stephen chose an apple-colored" balloon and Frances took "a pale green one," perhaps representing the apple tasted by Adam and Eve and the green fig leaves they used to cover themselves. Stephen and Frances are still in paradise: "Between them on the bench lay a tumbled heap of delights still to come." Frances—her name can be, with a slight change of spelling, masculine or feminine—brags of a beautiful long silver balloon she had once had (the images become phallic in this scene), but Stephen urges her to go on playing with the round ones. He feels his ribs and is surprised that they stop in front—a playful reference to Adam's lost rib. Frances grows tired and restless, Stephen pushes the "limp objects" toward her, urging her to accept the delights at hand, the millions more to come. Instead, she wants other delights: "a stick" of licorice to make "liquish" water. Stephen has no money, but Frances is persistent; she is thirsty and might have to return home. To keep her, Stephen promises to make lemonade. He takes the forbidden fruit and makes the drink, putting it into a teapot; to keep the adults (God) from knowing, Stephen suggests they go to the back garden, behind the rose bushes. Frances runs beside him like a deer, "her face wise with knowledge," as Stephen carries the teapot. They drink from the spout of the teapot—a phallic image in keeping with her rejection of limp balloons and request for a licorice stick—playing games and letting the lemonade run over them. They give the rosebush a drink, and Stephen baptizes it in the "Name father son holygoat," paganizing the Christian ceremony.

Caught by the servants, Frances looks at her shoes and lets Stephen take the blame. In this scene Stephen leaves babyhood, and innocence; his route parallels the Old Testament journey of humanity, expelled from the garden but free to follow strange gods.

Uncle David is angry about the theft of the balloons, calls the boy a thief, and rails against Stephen's father. The grandmother makes no real attempt to protect the boy; she calls him "Grandma's darling," but agrees with David that he should be sent home.

Stephen's mother arrives, quarrels with her mother and brother in a histrionic scene, and promises to come for a visit in a few days. Stephen, stripped of his innocence, does not want to go home to his father, but his mother carries him to the car. In the front seat, alone and frightened, without love or comfort, initiated into the ways of the world, Stephen sings to himself a little refrain: "I hate Papa, I hate Mama, I hate Grandma, I hate Uncle David, I hate Old Janet, I hate Marjory, I hate Papa, I hate Mama." He starts the song over again but does not mention Frances. The story ends, however, not with this terrible song, but with Stephen growing sleepy, resting his head on his mother's knee. She draws him closer; he could be her love; she drives with one hand, holding Stephen closely with the other.

The martyr Stephen, in the sixth and seventh chapters of Acts, reminded the multitudes that they would not accept the message brought by Jesus, that they always persecuted the prophets. True to his prediction, he was stoned to death. Porter's Stephen is also martyred; he is driven into exile just as Joyce's Stephen is, just as Wescott was, just as Porter was.

"**Theft.**" When Matthew Josephson's wife learned about her husband's affair with Porter, she gave him an ultimatum: choose between wife and mistress. Josephson chose his wife, but attempted to stay on friendly terms with Porter. Porter felt great pain and humiliation, and her story "Theft" makes direct use of this failed love affair. [12]

One of Porter's most subtle and complicated stories, "Theft" (1929), is told from the point of view of a no-longer young writer, who supports herself largely by writing reviews. [13] The central character has much in common with the unnamed, alienated narrator in "Hacienda." The setting is the New York bohemian world, perhaps in the 1920s; the characters are insecure and poor; and the mood is sad, gloomy, and dismal. In the opening scene, the lateness of the hour, the desolate elevated station, and the driving rain set the tone.

The writer begins retracing in her mind the events surrounding the loss of her purse. She asserts the clearness of her memory and the value she placed on the purse: she had put it on the wooden bench the night before and had dried it. The next day she realizes it is gone, and thinks back to the previous evening. Camilo, a graceful young Spanish acquaintance, had walked her to the elevated station in the rain, ruining his new, biscuit-colored hat. She sees Camilo as one who uses most effectively the small courtesies but ignores "the larger and more troublesome ones." Somewhat intoxicated, her thoughts focus on the impractical hat, that it would now look shabby; and she compares Camilo's hat with Eddie's— always old, but worn with "careless and incidental rightness." But she has no intimate relationship with Camilo, no real concern for him. She sees him at the corner putting his hat under his overcoat and feels that "she had betrayed him by seeing."

Before she can get to the elevated, Roger calls to her; they are old friends and perhaps lovers; he readily admits the bulge under his coat is his hat being protected—the hats help reveal the characters of the three men—and she willingly shares a taxi with him. Stopped at a light, she sees, and in her recollection comments on, two scenes: three young men, in "seedy snappy-cut suits and gay neckties" arguing about love and marriage; and two girls, in transparent raincoats, whose worlds are, in a way, transparent to her.

They are saying, "Yes, I know all about *that*. But what about me? You're always so sorry for *him*." She sees them not as humans: the boys are scarecrows and the girls rush by on "pelican legs."

Later, Roger tells her that Stella is returning, that all of their differences are "settled." She says she had had a letter too, but things had been settled for her. He borrows a dime to help pay for the fare, and tells her to take aspirin and a hot bath to ward off a cold.

Upstairs, she visits Bill, a self-centered, weak writer, who lacks the outer strength of Camilo and the inner strength of Roger. He complains about paying alimony, is oblivious to the fate of his child, and refuses to pay her fifty dollars promised for her help on his play. She lets him steal her money without a real objection. Downstairs in her own apartment, she reads again the letter from her previous lover—the letter that had settled things for her—a letter accusing her of destroying his love for her (shifting the blame from himself to her). She tears the letter into strips, demonstrating clearly that her alienation from those around her springs from herself. In destroying the letter she destroys her last link with her estranged lover, presumably Eddie.

She then remembers the events of the next morning: the janitress comes in while she is having a bath, and sometime later goes out, "closing the door very sharply." Then the purse is gone. She dresses and makes coffee, her excitement and anger growing. She puts the cup down in the center of the table (as if in a religious ritual) and descends into the basement to demand her purse from the janitress, who is at the furnace and streaked with coal dust. The scene that follows is of an inferno. The woman first denies stealing the gold-cloth purse. The writer attempts to reassert herself, to act positively, instead of giving in, as she had with Bill. As she confronts the janitress, she remembers that she had never worried about possessions, that she had been indifferent and careless with them, that she had not loved them just as she had not loved or been able to go on loving others: she had given others the chance to rob her. The physical act of this theft becomes a symbol to her: "she felt that she had been robbed of an enormous number of valuable things, whether material or intangible: things lost or broken by her own fault, things she had forgotten and left in houses when she moved: books borrowed from her and not returned, journeys she had planned and had not made, ... the long patient suffering of dying friendships and the dark inexplicable death of love"; all these she has lost and is losing again in memory. Her anger over the theft of the purse and her desire to get it back have been a desperate effort to keep from losing herself, an unconscious assumption of blame and responsibility for her own losses.

The janitress returns the purse, saying, with "red fire flickering in her eyes," that she had a niece who needed a pretty purse, a niece who was young and needed her chance, that the writer had already had hers. The writer tries to return the purse to the janitress, who says spitefully that the niece does not need it because she is young and pretty: "I guess you need it worse than she does!" The writer is then caught in a circular trap; she seems again to be causing her own alienation, her own losses. The janitress has the last word: the purse is being stolen from the niece.

The writer puts the purse on the table (the altar), but the coffee (sacrament) is chilled, and she knows that "I was right not to be afraid of any thief but myself, who will end by leaving me nothing." The story's incidents are carefully chosen to emphasize this final view. The theme of alienation is pointed up by the rain, and its effects on Camilo, Roger, and the writer; she sees that the rain changes the shape of everything. Stairs would have taken her to the elevated (and the life of the spirit); instead she descended into the basement, a trip into a heart of darkness, where she saw the fire-filled eyes of the janitress and had the first intimations of the real nature of the theft.

The primary symbol in the story, and its unifying theme, is the purse and the woman's feelings about it. At first, it is a material possession, a birthday present probably from her lover, Eddie, representing their past relationship and its dissolution. At the beginning of the story the purse is almost empty, for she is both physically and spiritually poor. The janitress forces her to take back the purse, but she no longer wants it; she has physical possession of what she had lost, but is haunted by other, symbolic losses. This final irony is perhaps the most bitter, for she sees her own tragedy and that of all people as the tragedy of self-betrayal.

The search for love, both profane and sacred, is an important theme of this complex story. The narrator rejects Camilo, loses Roger to his wife, is cheated by Bill, and rejected by Eddie. She is left with a gold purse and cold coffee, a wasteland figure without any kind of love.

The Irish Stories

"**The Cracked Looking-Glass.**" During her brief marriage to Ernest Stock, Porter lived in a house in Connecticut owned by Genevieve Taggard and her husband. A former tenant in the house, Givner reports, was a "rich Irish widow . . . who had caused something of a scandal with her pier-glass mirror, her big carved bed, and the young boys she adopted for no good purpose."[14] Porter took that germ of an idea, and utilizing her knowledge of Joyce and her own propensities for young men (one of whom she had just married), transformed it into a fine story.

Stephen Dedalus said of the mirror Buck Mulligan stole from a servant: "It is a symbol of Irish art. The cracked looking-glass of a servant." Joseph Wiesenfarth has pointed out, in "Illusion and Allusion: Reflections in 'The Cracked Looking-Glass,' " that the mirror symbol in Porter's story is a reference not only to Joyce, since its character Rosaleen had formerly been a chambermaid and practiced the Irish art of self-deception, but also to Tennyson's Lady of Shallot who wove her web while observing through a mirror the life outside the tower. Likewise, Rosaleen observes herself through a mirror and often works on a tablecloth that apparently will never be completed. Porter may also have had in mind 1 Corinthians, chapter 13, verse 12: "For now we see through a glass, darkly: but then face to face." Wiesenfarth in his perceptive study sees that the mirror symbol, central to the story, changes constantly, encompassing "the imagination of Rosaleen, the imperfection of human love, the necessity of accepting that love as it is, the marriage of Rosaleen and Dennis, reality, the difficulty of knowing reality."

"The Cracked Looking-Glass" (1932) is filled with Joycean techniques and allusions.[15] Rosaleen is an Irish woman who, like Molly Bloom, is married to a man no longer sexually satisfying to her; like Molly, she has had a son who died; and without son, without husband-lover, she has taken literally or in spirit other lovers. It is not quite certain how many young boys she has had in the house; Kevin had been with them for a year but had gone away when Rosaleen became jealous after seeing his young girl friend's picture. Rosaleen asks Hugh Sullivan to come live with them, but he declares it too dangerous. And a neighbor extends the whole field of promiscuity: "A pretty specimen you are, Missis O'Toole, with your old husband and the young boys in your house and the traveling salesmen and the drunkards lolling on your doorstep all hours—" Although one sees events and characters from the point of view of both Rosaleen and her husband Dennis, the reader never finds any final statement, never reaches an absolute truth.

The story is an account of Rosaleen's progression from illusion to reality. Thirty years younger than Dennis and sexually deprived, Rosaleen tries to make the grim reality of her existence more endurable by "embroidering," Irish fashion, the stories she tells. The story opens with an account of her Billy-cat and his death, which she says she learned of in a dream. Dennis, who considers himself "a sober, practical, thinking man, a lover of truth," shows the story to be a fabrication, but his opinion, to Rosaleen at least, is suspect because like Mr. Bloom, he is an outsider: he had grown up not in Ireland but in Bristol, England. As observer, Dennis has other weaknesses: he is filled with self-pity and he cannot see that Rosaleen had changed in the twenty-five years they had been married.

Dennis lives almost entirely in the present, while Rosaleen lives much in the past, which she can more easily improve upon in memory and in story. She thinks of her girlhood in Ireland as a time of great and triumphant pleasures, and she still longs for men to fight over her. Instead of this glorious green past, she has in reality a farm in Connecticut, an old husband growing senile, and her own fading looks. In her dreams, she achieves a measure of triumph by having others die: she dreams that Kevin, the house-painter, does not write because he is dead; she dreams the Irish boy she could have married is dead. When the great-grandfather dies and she has to face actual death, she puts aside the grim reality by dreaming about it.

The most important episode of the story, the one that shocks Rosaleen back to reality, is her trip to Boston to see her sister Honora, who she dreams is dying. The dream gives her a chance to escape from her grim life on the farm, a pretext for an adventure away from the small village. But she does not go directly to Boston; she goes by way of New York, where she lived with Dennis when he was a headwaiter at a hotel, and she stops there to see two romantic films: *The Prince of Love* and *The Lover King*.

In Boston, she discovers her sister has moved without leaving an address, dramatic proof that her dream about her sister was not true. She is forced to abandon another dream when the young Irishman Hugh Sullivan, either understanding exactly or completely misunderstanding, refuses her invitation to come to the farm. Her dream of having a young man in the house unfulfilled and all her other dreams shattered, she is left with the reality of living out her life with Dennis.

As she forgets her old dreams, she also forgets to buy a new looking-glass, and with her acceptance of the old glass, she accepts her life and marriage. Life is "a mere dream," she thinks, accepting that too; and she puts aside the dreams of the green field of her youth. She asks Dennis why he married her, and he replies that he could not have done better. Suddenly, she feels solicitous, wants him to keep warmer, and says she does not know what will happen to her when he is gone. Dennis turns from the reality of his death, saying, "Let's not think of it," and she agrees not to, ending compassionately, "I could cry if you crooked a finger at me." Rosaleen has accepted the reality of their life, but neither can face the future, his approaching death. The story ends on the same note of despair for the human condition that one finds in many of Porter's other stories, but the poetic Irish language, the realistic details, and the literary echoes are superbly intertwined in this skillfully written, complex story.

"A Day's Work." "A Day's Work" (1940) was written in 1937 in New York soon after Porter's husband had left for a position in South America.[16] Her third marriage was failing and soon would end. She had been particularly distressed because her husband Pressly had not been able to make up his mind about jobs, for which she considered him weak and vacillating. Against this personal background, Porter fashioned a story based, as Givner notes, "on a family's quarrels which she overheard through the air vent of the Perry Street Apartment."[17]

"A Day's Work" is more than a story of the battle of the sexes or another of Porter's investigations of marriage, as some critics have seen it. It has as its setting the slums of New York during the depression, and as social background the political corruption of Tammany Hall. Mr. Halloran, an aging Irish immigrant, from whose point of view we see much of the story, has been fired from his job in a grocery store two years before his retirement, ostensibly because of the depression but more likely so his employer can avoid paying a pension. For seven years he has been sitting at home, drawing his relief money and listening to the complaints of Mrs. Halloran, who adds to their income by doing washing and ironing.

As cantankerous as she, he is always talking back, constantly provoking his shrewish wife. He is particularly bitter because he had wanted to go into politics—and the closely allied numbers racket—but his wife would not allow it. McCorkery, the political boss, had predicted that Mrs. Halloran would hold Halloran down, but in doing so she had kept him out of the rackets.

Mrs. Halloran, puritanically religious, had disapproved of McCorkery and his fast crowd but had approved of Connolly, a good Catholic with nine children. Halloran learns from a policeman that Connolly is wanted by the G-men because of his criminal activities; Halloran, completely amoral, objects to police meddling, and the policeman, corrupted by the system, wants to know what the harm was: "A man must get his money from somewhere when he's in politics. They oughta give him a chance." On the way to the saloon, Halloran imagines what his life might have been like if his wife had let him work with McCorkery, and he dreams of what it will be like to talk with McCorkery again, telling him of his dismal home life and his willingness to help get out the votes in the upcoming election.

The dream and the reality come together violently at the bar. McCorkery is there, but Halloran does not ask for a job. After seeing the prosperous political boss, Halloran becomes even more depressed by what might have been; he drinks too much, and drops the whiskey bottle—reminiscent of the opening scene of Joyce's "Grace." McCorkery, needing votes, is outwardly calm when dealing with his old crony who is a failure; his voice is loud and hearty but has a curse in it; he slips money to Halloran and sends him home by taxi.

At home, Halloran is repulsed by his wife. She appears in his alcohol-induced state as a ghost in a "faded gingham winding sheet," and her voice is "thick with grave damp." He throws the iron at the "devil" advancing toward him and then flees into the street and tells a policeman he has killed his wife. Before the police can investigate, Mrs. Halloran appears and tells the policeman she had fainted and struck her head on the ironing board. She helps her husband upstairs, throws him on the bed, wets a large towel, ties knots in the end, and begins to strike him in the face, at each whack calling out his offenses: drunkenness, stealing, walking in his stockinged feet, and "for your daughter and your part in her." (The scene is remarkably similar to the *Ship of Fools* scene in which Mrs. Treadwell strikes Denny in the face with her shoe.) As a symbol of her victorious assault, she winds the wet towel about her head, knot over her shoulder, puts the money from McCorkery in her locked metal box, and calls her daughter to announce, for the neighbors to hear, that Halloran has a job. All her objections to the political boss have disappeared.

Illusion and reality clash forcefully and ironically in this sordid, black comedy, filled with mellifluous Irish phrases. Porter manages to capture the sterile, hate-filled lives of the Hallorans, and she brilliantly etches in the political machinations of two Tammany leaders, the corruption of the ward itself, and the corrosive effects of the depression. She presents, as Marjorie Ryan has shown in "*Dubliners* and the Stories of Katherine Anne Porter," the "strange, violent life in a society as dead on the surface as Joyce's."

The psychological probings and rhetorical dialogue are especially noteworthy, and this realistic story of life in the New York slums during the depression deserves to be better known.

German Stories

"Holiday." The aristocratic Hans in "The Leaning Tower" announces that when he speaks of Germans, he does not mean peasants; Tadeusz the Pole replies, "Perhaps we should always mean peasants when we speak of a race . . . the peasant stays in his own region and marries his own kind, generation after generation, and creates the race." Porter presents such a race in the Müller family, third-generation Americans, but still German peasants.

"Holiday" grew out of a visit Porter and her sister made to a German farm.[18] It was a period of great stress for Porter, for her first marriage was in trouble and she was soon to bolt from it. She finished a draft of the story in 1924, wrote three different versions of the ending, and then set the story aside. It was found decades later and finally published in 1960.[19]

The story is told by an unnamed narrator who recalls the events long after they happened. The sensibilities and the background of the narrator are Porter's, and she states the thesis in the first paragraph: the narrator is too young for the troubles she is having, and her family background and training have not taught her that it is possible to run away from some things. She had learned later the difference between courage and foolhardiness; but, when the events of the story had taken place, she did not then know "that we do not run from the troubles and dangers that are truly ours, and it is better to learn what they are earlier than later, and if we don't run from the others, we are fools."

Wishing to escape her problems, which with the passage of time had diminished and need not be described, the narrator had gone, on the recommendation of her school friend Louise, to the east Texas farm of the Müllers. Louise had described the family and the farm romantically, but the reality that confronted the narrator is quite different. Left on "the sodden platform of a country station," she is taken in a dilapidated wagon through bleak country to a forbidding farmhouse, set in an infertile spot. The fat puppy of Louise's story has turned into an enormous, detestable beast.

When she arrives at the front door, the whole family, except the father, comes out, and the narrator sees that they all have the same eyes, the same "taffy-colored hair," even though two were sons-in-law. She finds herself in a patriarchal society, in which Papa Müller and the men are treated with deference and respect, the wives standing behind their husbands at meal times to fill their plates.

The story moves slowly, as the narrator observes the customs of this farming family with its deep roots in the soil. Staunchly conservative, almost completely isolated from the mainstream of American life—in fact from most community life except for Saturday excursions to the *Turnverein*—the family forms its own little closed society. The narrator notes with irony that Papa Müller is a student of Marx and yet is the richest member of the community. She observes the disciplined children at play, and a wedding, a birth, and a funeral—the life cycle of the family.

All the realistic details (the story is filled with animals and animal imagery) suddenly take on more meaning when the narrator discovers that Ottilie, the crippled, dumb servant girl, is actually one of the Müller children. Ottilie works constantly, as if she were in perfect health, preparing the vast quantities of food consumed by the family: she works because the work has to be done, and because she can do it. John Hagopian in *Insight I* speculates that in naming Ottilie "Miss Porter had in mind the Ottilie Home for Crippled Children in New York (an obvious juxtaposition of *Ottilie* and *Crippled*) named after the saint in Alsace, who was born blind but whose sight was restored on baptism." Ottilie shows the narrator a picture of herself as a healthy little girl, tries to speak, but cannot. Ottilie's past is frozen in the picture, but as she and the narrator look at it, the picture brings the two of them together. For a moment, the narrator thinks, Ottilie knew she was Ottilie, "knew she suffered," as she staggered away, significantly leaving the picture face downward. Later that day, Ottilie regards the narrator as a stranger, but the narrator cannot let Ottilie remain so.

In immediate contrast to the family's relationship with Ottilie is a long account of their treatment of animals: the boys trap wild animals, the girls care for the animals and chickens tenderly, Frau Müller dies as a result of her overexertions in tending the animals during a storm. The Müllers had put Ottilie out of mind, the narrator thinks, (though this may not be entirely true), and, out of self-defense, they forget her.

The narrator's compassion for Ottilie is shown with great restraint and is contrasted with scenes of the Müllers' intense emotions after the death of Mrs. Müller. Even Ottilie is caught up in the emotionalism; the narrator, who stays alone in her room on the day of the funeral, filled with the "terror of dying," hears strange noises, and finds Ottilie howling in the kitchen. The narrator hitches horse to wagon and with Ottilie starts after the funeral procession, but they are too far behind, and there is no hope that Ottilie can be made a member of the family for that day; nor is there even any certainty that Ottilie wants to join the family circle.

Something, perhaps the sky or the turning wheels—the narrator never knows—suddenly fills Ottilie with joy. It is definitely spring, the flood has caused a profusion of vegetation (certainly the Müllers could understand only in a literal sense that April is the cruelest month), and they sit, horse stopped, surveying the woods and the heavens. The narrator ponders her mistake: "There was nothing I could do for Ottilie, selfishly as I wished to ease my heart of her; she was beyond my reach as well as any other human reach, and yet, had I not come nearer to her than I had to anyone else in my attempt to deny and bridge the distance between us, or rather, her distance from me?" She knows they are both fools of life, both fugitives from death, and, as a celebration, they have taken a holiday together. Ottilie becomes fidgety during their pause, and they start again, taking "the small road divided from the main traveled one." The irony is especially heavy as the narrator thinks to herself that they will be home in time for Ottilie to prepare supper and nobody need know of their excursion.

The meaning of the story, John Hagopian says in *Insight I*, "is simply this: that man lives in a universe without shape or meaning. He is therefore obligated to project a meaning, to shape and form his own life in an effort that is ultimately doomed since it will end with death and chaos. But while he is making the effort, he can be sustained by love—even love for a twisted, mute, half-beast of a human being like Ottilie. Since we are all prisoners of the universe together, let us love one another." Richard Poirier, in his introduction to *Prize Stories 1962: The O. Henry Awards* ("Holiday" won first prize), has a reading far different from Hagopian's. To Poirier, "The story is about people whose communal labor has created relationships among them and between them and their natural environment, so close that literally nothing except death can disrupt them."

The Müllers have given Ottilie an importance in the household, a central position; but they have forgotten their blood ties, their spiritual ties to her. Their treatment of her is at the same time cruel and practical. Neither Christianity nor Marxism has taught the Müllers compassion. One can, then, read "Holiday" as a political parable, as Porter's probing of the German question: she describes German clannishness, materialism, cruelty, love of animals and mistreatment of fellow human beings, a willingness to put out of mind the unpleasantness of the past—characteristics she also describes in "The Leaning Tower" and *Ship of Fools*. Whether read as personal narrative or as political parable, the conclusion is a sobering one: the narrator, although giving Ottilie a holiday, can do little for the girl, for the narrator's own holiday would end soon; she would leave the Müller farm, leave Ottilie and the Müllers to their fate, as she goes on to hers.

"The Leaning Tower." "The Leaning Tower" (1941) is set in Berlin at the time Porter lived there in 1931–32, and in the story she used many people she knew and events she witnessed or experienced.[20] For instance when she and Pressly were looking over a pension, Pressly touched a fragile replica of the Leaning Tower of Pisa and it crumbled. As Givner notes, Porter then lashed out at him: "Why must you touch things? Why must you always touch and destroy things?"[21] Porter herself appears as the central character Charles Upton, and his friend Kuno is based on her childhood friend Erna Schlemmer. One can properly ask why Porter assumed the persona of a male. Givner thinks it "possibly reflects her identification with Eugene Pressly during the Berlin period."[22]

Many of the characters in the story are named for people Porter met in Berlin, but with their characteristics sometimes changed. For instance, she rather liked her own landlady, but Rosa Reichl in the story becomes a disagreeable tyrant. In other instances, Porter seems to have used characteristics of other people she had known, as in the character of Tadeusz Mey who takes on fragments from the life of Joseph Retinger, one of Porter's lovers in Mexico during the early 1920s.[23]

Some journal notes Porter made in December 1931 are also useful for understanding the background of her story. A young poet she knew in Berlin objected that she should not bother reading Rilke's *Elegies*: "He belongs to the old romantic soft-headed Germany that has been our ruin. The new Germany is hard, strong, we will have a new race of poets, tough and quick, like your prize fighters." The poet gave Porter some of his poems, and she found that the "words were tough and the rhythms harsh, the ideas all the most grossly brutal; and yet, it was vague weak stuff in the end."[24]

In another note she describes a conversation with L. [unidentified] and von G. [Göring] about Nietzsche: "Nietzsche is dangerous because his mind has power without intelligence; he is all will without enlightenment. His phrases are inflated, full of violence, a gross kind of cruel poetry—like Wagner's music. They both throw a hypnotic influence over their hearers. But I could always resist hypnotists. When I think of Nietzsche and Wagner . . . I find charlatans. . . . And madness. In Nietzsche's case . . . his diseased brain gave his style the brilliancy of a rotting fish. L. and von G. worship them both with a religious awe."[25] In 1941 she captured, in her short novel, much of the spirit of that impression and rumination of 1931.

In 1932, still in Berlin, Porter wrote that R. [not otherwise identified] was a man filled with maliciousness, one who spoke evil of everyone, and he told her that she could know nothing of the higher levels of religious experience because "Religious experience belongs exclusively to the masculine principle." Without seeing the irony of his words, he assured her that "Only ample, generous natures are capable of the love of God."[26] Porter reflected some of these philosophical, religious, and aesthetic statements in "The

Leaning Tower," and she also incorporates the malignity she saw in German society that she was writing about in her journal in 1931 and 1932.

The story may be divided into five major parts: the café as a place of memory, of Charles's childhood illusions of Germany and the reality he now sees; the search for a new room and the exit from the hotel; the new room and the inhabitants of the pension; the night club; and the final revelation in the room. Charles Upton, from whose point of view we see the events, is given a background similar to Porter's. Sensitive but, like Miranda, naive, he came from a central Texas farming family with Kentucky ties; and he had, against the initial wishes of his family, been interested in art—just as Porter, against the wishes of her family, had determined to be a writer. He had come to Berlin largely because of his boyhood friendship with Kuno Hillentafel, who had died on a trip to his homeland and whose mother was alleged to have been a countess. Through a romantic projection of Kuno's descriptions, Charles had imagined Berlin to be a great city of castles towering in the mists.

Alone in the strange city that Christmas season, left with his memories of Kuno, Charles finds Berlin depressing as he sits in the café. Among the heavy buildings are heavy, piglike people or slim young students all dressed alike; he had seen in his few days in the city the desperate poverty of the country, the streetwalkers, the beggars. His impressions had been harsh and poignant. The shock of being in a strange city and culture have robbed him even of sexual desire, and he has been unable to show interest in the streetwalkers. His impressions are not ordered; his is not a reflective mind, and he cannot generalize about the German society he finds so disturbing. He is storing his impressions for his drawings, which can be brutally accurate, as when he sketches the hotel owners: the woman as a sick fox and the man as half-pig, half-tiger. Charles's isolation is total, and the larger the crowd he finds himself in, the more isolated he becomes.

The rush of impressions subsides as Charles sets out to search for a room, for the rooms fall into an easily distinguished pattern of stuffy, faded elegance or expensive modernity. At the apartment of Frau Rosa Reichl—she had once been rich, had employed many servants, but now lives in reduced but not poverty-stricken circumstances—he accidentally breaks a plaster souvenir of the Leaning Tower of Pisa, a tottering structure in actuality and, in replica, a fitting symbol of a society soon itself to fall. Frau Reichl is aware of the significance of Charles's blunder. Outwardly she sees the fragile souvenir as a memento of her honeymoon, but it had also come to be a symbol of her cherished past. Charles can see that she regrets having left it out for crude foreigners to touch.

When Charles announces his intentions of leaving the hotel where he has been staying, the hotel owners lose all civility. He is outrageously overcharged, threatened with police action if he protests the bill, and intimidated by passport inspection—he had been told he would feel like a criminal in Germany.

The outward bestiality disappears once he moves into Rosa's room. On the day of his move, he learns, in a quiet scene in a barber shop, that a shouting politician (obviously Hitler) had made one particular hair style popular. This third section of the story presents Rosa's apartment and the inhabitants as a microcosm of German society in 1931, but since Porter includes only three Germans, one American, and one Pole, her cast is limited. Charles says of Rosa and the guests: "They were all good people, they were in terrible trouble, jammed up together in this little flat with not enough air or space or money, not enough of anything, no place to go, nothing to do but gnaw each other." Charles has the best room and pays the most rent because Americans are thought to be rich. This mythic wealth also protects him from Rosa's sharp tongue, but her favorite in the house is Hans von Gehring (Porter's name for Hermann Goering), an aristocratic-looking young man, a student at Heidelberg, where he had fought a duel and is now receiving treatment for his infected wound. Charles wants to like the young man, but he is unable to comprehend a society that admires such barbaric acts. He rejects the wound and everything that allows such behavior, even though he had seen the antique dueling pistols of his own great-grandfather. Hans is proud of his scar, often fingers it, and Charles sees in the young man's face his true nature: "amazing arrogance, pleasure, inexpressible vanity and self-satisfaction."

Rosa's scapegoat is Herr Otto Bussen, a Platt Deutsch, whose inferior social station and poverty give Rosa license to intimidate and demean him at every opportunity. That he is a brilliant student at the university makes no difference to Frau Reichl. When Herr Bussen poisons himself, accidentally or otherwise, she is as concerned about her rugs as about his health.

The other lodger, Tadeusz Mey, a Polish-Austrian pianist and a cosmopolitan at home in London and Paris, is living in Berlin because there is a good teacher there. Mey is aware of the evils in society and opposes them, but he is cynical enough to study and live in a corrupt German society.

In a dream Charles's premonitions about the society, as personified by the house and its inhabitants, surface vividly. The house is burning, pulsing with fire. Charles walks from the building with all the paintings he would ever do in his life. When he turns to look back, he thinks at first that they have all escaped, but he hears a ghostly groan and sees no one. Symbolically Charles knows that he could and would walk away from a society that was destroying itself and its members. His artistic creations are more important to him than any attempt to save the unsavable, to save those who, we must assume, would misunderstand his act and turn on him ferociously. Charles does not reflect on his dream when he wakens, stifling in the feather coverlets, and he does not think of it when he considers giving an extra coat to Herr Bussen, an act that Mey says would be a great mistake.

The story then moves from the rooming house to a newly opened, middle-class bar where the young men go to celebrate the New Year. In many ways, this section confirms Tadeusz's view that losing the war damaged the "nation's personality," but it goes beyond that to search for personality traits that were established long before the war. At the night club, Charles sees a variety of Germans in a social setting: Lutte, a thin, blonde model, to Hans a perfect German type; a large barmaid, attractive to Herr Bussen; two movie stars; and a large crowd of noisy, sentimental revelers.

As the conversation swirls on into a long discussion of races and cultures, fat Otto, an aspiring intellectual, insists that "the true great old Germanic type is lean and tall and fair as gods." Charles, who like Miranda has rejected the mythic view of a "splendid past" that his parents had taught him, cannot compete in the conversation since he knows almost no history. Drawn into the gaiety of the night, he dances with Lutte, but finds that she is interested in him only if he can get her to Hollywood. She soon turns her attention to the more aristocratic Hans. Tadeusz speaks of his family, which has lived in the same house for eight centuries, of the stifling society of his childhood, of the anti-Semitic attitudes implicit in religious dogma; his memories of the past are mixed, "something between a cemetery and a Lost Paradise." Otto, who grew up in a Lutheran family, speaks of his dismal childhood, of building his life on a romantic view of Luther, and of his apparent willingness to follow anyone he sees as great.

At midnight, nobody notices the irony when a wooden cuckoo announces the New Year. A toast is drunk, a "disordered circle formed," and there is much singing and drunken revelry until "the circle broke up, ran together, whirled, loosened, fell apart." This tourists' Germany of lighthearted gaiety cannot last, and the young men have to get the drunken Otto home, his befuddled moribund state symbolic of the German intellectual. As he is carried past Rosa, she looks at her young men fondly. In his drunken state Charles sees (or thinks he sees) the Leaning Tower, now repaired, behind the glass door of the cabinet, and he knows he can crush again the frail, useless thing—it is "a whimsical pain in the neck . . . yet [it] had some kind of meaning" that tries to break into his consciousness but cannot. He feels a "desolation of the spirit" because he is beginning to see that the society is going to fall, that it will involve him, and that there is nothing he will do. "He didn't feel sorry for himself," but he does know that "no crying jag or any other kind of jag would ever, in this world, do anything at all for him."

The story has many brilliantly conceived scenes; it is not the failure that many critics have found it to be. Charles has vague portents of the meaning of what he sees; in his dream, he realizes the society is facing destruction, and he has learned that his initial reaction to the Germans is true: "They were the very kind of people that Holbein, Dürer and Urs Graf had drawn . . . their late-medieval faces full of hallucinated malice and a kind of sluggish but intense cruelty that worked its way up from their depths slowly through the layers of helpless gluttonous fat."

"The Germans," Porter said in an interview in the 31 March 1962 *Saturday Review,* "are against anybody and everybody, and they haven't changed a bit." She never believed reconciliation with the German people was possible. In "The Leaning Tower" she was engaged in an early literary probing of the German problem, of the nature and meaning of evil; she was to continue that study in *Ship of Fools.*

Each of these stories contains autobiographical material and each is an investigation of what Porter has rightly called the "terrible failure of the life of man in the Western world." Her aim as a writer, she says, was "to tell a straight story," and she succeeded admirably. These stories, set in the South, in New England, in New York, and in Germany, and dealing with poor whites, Irish-Americans, artists, Berliners, German peasants, and many others are a remarkable literary achievement. They are as subtle and perceptive and masterful as the best works of Joyce or James.

Chapter Five
Ship of Fools

Known by the earlier working titles of "Promised Land," "The Land That Is Nowhere," and "No Safe Harbor," *Ship of Fools* was for years the subject of much literary gossip. The novel was often promised but always postponed, and many critics gave up hope that it would ever appear. Glenway Wescott in *Images of Truth* said that Porter set out to create "a large lifelike portrayal of a numerous and representative society, with contrasts of the classes and the masses and the generations and the ethnic groups, with causes and effects in the private psychology of one and all, and with their influences on one another—every man to some extent a part of every other man's fate—and all of this made manifest in behavior, action, plot!" Wescott wrote of the tribulations that beset Porter during the years she was writing *Ship of Fools*: unfavorable destiny, "passionate life and personal weakness and disadvantages in the day and age and in our present heterodox American culture." To these one should certainly add Porter's need to support herself by lecturing in colleges and universities across the country and, perhaps, her fear of publishing a long work.

Even some of Porter's friends lost faith in the novel, as she continued working on it over the years, publishing not the work itself but fragments of it in *Harper's*, *Atlantic Monthly*, the *Texas Quarterly* and many other journals—fragments that did not and could not show the scope of her novel. At one time, Wescott wrote, but did not mail, a letter suggesting to Porter that she give up the project, salvage what sketches she could, and move on to other work.

The story, based on Porter's 1931 voyage to Germany, was to have been included as a short novel in *Pale Horse, Pale Rider*, but she went on working on it and it kept on growing. There were interruptions—always interruptions—and promises to her publishers, but the novel remained a plan, with only small sections finished. She began serious work on it in Yaddo in 1941, and for the next fourteen years, she worked at it "a page here and there" until 1955, when she rented a house in Connecticut and put in three years of intense work. She wrote Glenway Wescott on 5 July 1956 that she was bored with her work, "because the plan is so finished, there is nothing to do but just type it down to the end, and OH GOD! how I have to beat myself over the head to get started every morning." But in the spring of 1961 she "finished the whole damn thing in six weeks."[1]

American Criticism

Porter's prepublication interviews in *Time* and *Newsweek* in July of 1961 were carefully controlled and made no mention of the problems and self-doubts hinted at by Wescott, but the stage was being set for her only popular success. Her short stories deservedly were widely praised, but the general reading public had never paid much attention to her works. The Book-of-the-Month Club, however, chose *Ship of Fools* as its April selection, and sent, in its brochure to members, a brief essay by Glenway Wescott (later published in expanded form in the *Atlantic Monthly* and in *Images of Truth*) and an ecstatic review by Clifton Fadiman, who declared, "here at last is Miss Porter's *magnum opus*. Not only was it worth waiting for, but your judges would be derelict in their duty if they did not wholeheartedly urge it upon the attention of Club members."

Book-of-the-Month-Club selection insured wide sales, and literary speculation and advance publicity contributed to the novel's becoming number one on the best-seller list within weeks of its publication on 12 April 1962. *Publisher's Weekly* for 21 May carried a note that the publishers, Atlantic-Little, Brown, had allocated over fifty thousand dollars for advertising the novel, including full page notices in the daily *New York Times* and in leading American magazines and newspapers and "360 60-second commercials" on FM radio stations.

Time informed its millions of readers, on 6 April 1962, that "*Ship of Fools* is a study in despair. The despair is not relieved by the usual dilutions. . . . In fact there are no personal obtrusions, nothing of the gracious, 70-year-old Southern gentlewoman who in the 20 years since her last book has seemed to occupy herself chiefly with being a charming chatterer at literary gatherings. Her testament is objective and her verdict is unemotional: the world is a place of foulness and fools."

Newsweek published an earlier but similar review on 2 April 1962:

"Among the lesser things to say about it is that it is the Book-of-the-Month for April. The main thing to declare is that in her full maturity, in a country where high-level fiction is scarce and likely to be fragile, Katherine Anne Porter has produced a work of rugged power and myriad insights, a book of the highest relevance to the bitterness and disruption of modern civilization."

Major American literary reviews were almost as laudatory. Mark Schorer in the lead article in the *New York Times Book Review* of 1 April 1962, (illustrated with a George Grosz drawing) noted the many delays in publication but concluded that the novel would endure "for many literary generations." Schorer's comprehensive, sympathetic review emphasized the influence of Brant's *Das Narrenschiff* on the novel, its artistic techniques, and its strongly developed characters, and concluded that *Ship of Fools* could best be compared "with the greatest novels of the past hundred years. Call it, for convenience, the 'Middlemarch' of a later day."

Louis Auchincloss, in a review in the *New York Herald-Tribune Books* on 1 April 1962, noted the novel's Victorian qualities. The review was illustrated with a flattering photograph of Porter by Bradford Bachrach. The issue also contained an interview by Maurice Dolbier, beginning with a Mexican toast, which Porter translated, "Health and money, more power to your elbow, many secret love affairs and time to enjoy them." The toast was enough to engage the reader's interest and to set the tone for Porter's chat on ancestors, writing, and men. She concluded, "I've had a very hard life, but it's not other people who have made it hard for me. I did that for myself. But I've had a good run for my money—a free field in the things that matter: the will to be an artist and to live as a human being."

Not all the early reviews were favorable; Granville Hicks, in *Saturday Review*, 31 March 1962, entered an early minority report: "It is hard not to judge the book in relation to the extended period of gestation; the temptation is to proclaim that it is either the fulfilment of a great hope or a sorry disappointment. But if it is certainly not the latter, neither is it quite the former. It shows that Miss Porter is one of the finest writers of prose in America. It also shows that she has mastered the form—or one of the forms—of the novel. On the other hand, it is something less than a masterpiece." His final conclusion was that "the novel, for all its lucidity and all

its insights, leaves the reader a little cold. There is in it, so far as
I can see, no sense of human possibility. Although we have known
her people uncommonly well, we watch unconcerned as, in the
curiously muted ending, they drift away from us." Accompanying
the review was a photograph of Porter posed glamorously, and an
interview by Rochelle Girson, in which Porter stated the theme of
her story: the novel, she said, is "the story of the criminal collusion
of good people—people who are harmless—with evil. It happens
through inertia, lack of seeing what is going on before their eyes.
I watched that happen in Germany and in Spain. I saw it with
Mussolini. I wanted to write about people in these predicaments—
really old predicaments with slightly new political and religious
aspects."

Porter's friend Josephine Herbst publicly and privately objected
to the novel. She wrote Alfred Kazin: "I never saw a bunch of more
unloving, irritable, touchy folks, either on ship or land." She also
objected to Porter's version of feminism, and to her ahistorical
treatment of Spaniards, Germans, and Americans.[2]

Howard Moss in the *New Yorker* for 28 April 1962, and Stanley
Kauffmann in the *New Republic,* 2 April 1962, also had reservations;
but the inevitable hostile reaction set in with Theodore Solotaroff's
" 'Ship of Fools' & the Critics" in *Commentary* for October 1962.
Solotaroff categorized what he saw as the central concerns of other
reviewers: the personality cult around Porter, the universality of the
novel, characters in the novel, and the general breakdown of society.
Then he set about to counter their generally favorable assessment
with his own view. He objected strenuously to Porter's presentation
of Herr Löwenthal, the Jew: "Miss Porter uses him in a situation
whose implications are both historically misleading and morally
vicious." In fact, he argued, Porter had presented "the stage Jew
of the modern literary tradition whom other Christian writers of
sensibility (among them T. S. Eliot) have dragged out of the ghetto
to represent the vulgar and menacing dislocations of traditional
order." German critics were later to take up the charge of unfairness,
but it was not the presentation of the Jew that annoyed them.
Solotaroff concluded that Porter had failed to present an allegory
of the "ship of this world on its voyage to eternity," that the
novel was, rather, a labored account of a tedious voyage, revealing
to the reader "little more than misanthropy and clever technique."

English and German Criticism

English critical reception of the novel was definitely cool. Robert Taubman, writing in the *Statesman* of 11 November 1962, complained that Porter had written a dull novel about folly: "the novel fails because it never gets down to more than marginal analysis." The fault lay in Porter's "resources as a writer," he concluded. "If she gets as far as folly and some minor brutalities, she doesn't get as far as evil."

The *Times Literary Supplement* review for 2 November 1962 admitted that there were moments of "great power and compassion" in the novel, but the review was generally unfavorable: "One may guess at what went wrong. Composed over twenty years, under the impact of a changing, darkening reality, *Ship of Fools* may have become to Miss Porter a complex argument, a provocation to constant technical virtuosity, rather than an imaginative whole. One cannot help wondering whether she *knows* enough—of German history, of the sources of modern anti-semitism, of European middle-class speech and values—or whether that knowledge has penetrated the exquisite, but very special, range of her feelings." The reviewer summed up many of the English critics' objections: "But the achievements are those of a great short-story writer. They glitter like passages of subtle, concentrated brushwork in a canvas too large and too thinly composed. And that may point to the essential flaw. The allegory Miss Porter has devised is too naive for the literal and moral enormity of her theme."

Sybille Bedford in the *Spectator* for 16 November 1962, praised the novel: "The Great American Novel has appeared; ironically, it has turned out to be a great universal novel." But there were also flaws: "the massed detail," the static quality of the novel, and a wavering attitude toward Mrs. Treadwell. Bedford's review, however, was the most sympathetic to appear in major English journals.

Angus Wilson, writing in the influential *Observer* on 28 October 1962, put the novel into the stereotyped formula of the 1930s: "It is impossible, I suspect, to use such a thumbed-over, middlebrow formula for writing a novel as the bringing together of passengers on a ship without awakening in the reader overtones of other, less-distinguished, novels that have exhausted the device, especially if, like Miss Porter, you lay your scene in the 1930s when that particular genre of book-club middlebrow novel was at its height."

German critics were even less kind, but in general their objections were political. Long before publication of a translation, reviews began to appear. The first, by Herbert von Borch in *Die Welt* of 9 June 1962, carried a preface by the editor who quoted Marguerite Higgins as saying that, while there was no anti-German movement in the United States, "understandable resentments" were still to be found. The editor concluded, "These resentments have found their expression in the voluminous, recently-published novel of a prominent American writer, 72-year-old Katherine Anne Porter, which was unusually successful with the critics and the public in the USA. Was this because of its theme or because of its literary qualities?" The headline over the review announced the answer to the question: " 'The Germans are still cruel, evil and fanatic' / Document of Hatred: K. A. Porter's 'Ship of Fools.' " Although Herbert von Borch's review was less virulent than the headline and in fact he did see some of the literary problems involved, he introduced a political interpretation that became a standard judgment of the work in Germany. Making use of the Girson interview in the 31 March 1962 *Saturday Review,* in which Porter emphasized that she had watched the rise of fascism in Europe but did not wish to write a thesis novel, von Borch chose instead to begin his quotation with Porter's views about Germany and the Germans: "they are just as dangerous as they were, and the moment they get back their power they are going to do it again. This complacency about Germany is simply horrifying. . . . The Germans have taken the Jews as a kind of symbol, but they are against anybody and everybody, and they haven't changed a bit!"

Sabina Lietzmann pursued this purely political interpretation in the *Frankfurter Allgemeine Zeitung* on 16 July 1962. Assuming the existence of a vast anti-German prejudice in America, she connected the novel with Shirer's study of the Third Reich and Stanley Kramer's movie *Judgment at Nuremberg,* works that also did not receive critical acclaim in Germany. Largely because Lietzmann failed to perceive the Brant framework of the novel, she saw only the German passengers as being treated extremely harshly. *Der Spiegel* on 12 September 1962 used much the same approach as Lietzmann's and concluded with an amazing standard of criticism: Porter was planning a European vacation to Ireland, Paris, and Rome, but "her route did not take her through Germany."

Heinz Paechter in "Miss Porter's New Garments," published in the *Deutsche Zeitung* of 13–14 October 1962, used, as part of his attack, Solotaroff's article in *Commentary*. Ignoring Solotaroff's objections to what he saw as Porter's unfair treatment of the Jew, Paechter wrote that Porter used the concept of the Nazi as a too-easy symbol of human depravity; he quoted Solotaroff as demonstrating that "out of her masochistic pessimism towards civilization, Miss Porter gives up every discrimination, and that this attitude makes her unable to characterize even the real Nazis in their depravity."

Norbert Muhlen in *Der Monat* for December 1962 found that, though it was indeed true that all nationalities were represented unflatteringly in the novel, the character portrayals were "the fashionable stereotyped image of humanity which affirms original sin but denies divine grace—an inevitable trade mark of 'sour kitsch' which no longer takes a rose-tinted but a murky view of the world." Muhlen complained that the German characters were clichés, and he objected to Porter's presenting Germans in 1931 talking of gas ovens, treating Jews as pariahs, or boycotting a German married to a Jew. Americans had to be told, he said, that about half of the Jewish marriages in 1931 were mixed marriages, and that, within the commercial society to which the character Freytag in the novel belonged, hardly anyone was discriminated against because of a Jewish wife.

While parts of German reviews were favorable, the troublesome political problem almost always predominated; German reviewers were unwilling to admit that any Germans were aboard the *Vera* in 1931.

Some Source Material and the Method

According to Glenway Wescott in *Images of Truth,* Porter said to him: "I promised myself solemnly: in this book [*Ship of Fools*] I will not load the dice. We all do it. . . . But this time, I resolved, everyone was to have his say. I would not take sides. I was on everyone's side." Wescott replied: "Yes, my dear, but it might also be said that you are on no one's side."

Asked about the unfavorable criticism of *Ship of Fools,* Porter said, "I wrote the book I meant to write." She went on to say, as reported in the *New York Herald-Tribune Books,* 11 October 1962, that she had always been gently treated by the critics but that, after her first best-seller, the critics "came at me with a double-barreled shotgun loaded with rock salt and carpet tacks, ready to let fly." They missed the point of the novel, she felt, and she said (with resignation or contempt; one cannot quite tell from the context), "I cannot do a thing for them."

Some of the critical confusion stemmed from Porter's own comments on the novel. German critics, faced with contradictory statements—her insistence that the theme of the novel was the collusion of good, harmless people with evil, and her assertion that Germans were just as evil and dangerous as they ever were—chose the latter and therefore interpreted the novel as propaganda. Mark Schorer agreed with Porter's often quoted comments that she had sympathy for her fools, but Solotaroff found her contemptuous of mankind and pointed not to her public statements but to the novel itself to argue his case. He was apparently unaware of Porter's personal anti-Semitism, which has been subsequently documented in Givner's biography.

Although Porter's accounts sometimes varied slightly, the general history of the composition is this: The novel began as a long letter to Caroline Gordon describing the passage from Mexico to Bremerhaven in 1931.[3] Porter continued during the 1930s to work on her notes about the journey, looking forward to a fictional account. She abandoned the original structure after she realized it would not be a short novel, but she kept the individual episodes, moving them about, and writing new scenes around them. The opening scene, she explained, remained the same, but she later added the dead boy; she had also written, in the first version, the last scene with the German boy calling out "Grüss Gott" as the ship docked in Bremerhaven. In an interview by Elizabeth Janeway for the *New York Times Book Review* of 1 April 1962, Porter explained the new structure: "The movement of the ship, forward, the movement of the waves, the movement of the passengers as they walk about the decks, all these got into the structure of the book. It moves in all these ways."

The significant sections of her long letter to Caroline Gordon are quoted in the Givner biography. The letter, now in the Caroline Gordon papers at the Princeton University Library, describes in detail many of the passengers on the German ship the S.S. *Werra*: the newlyweds ("If I ever saw two persons walking in Eden, it is now."); a huge fat man in steerage (he was transformed into the false revolutionary); the Zarzuela company; a hunchback; a large numer of German men and many fat German wives; an oculist from Texas (who was a model for Denny); a mad Cuban woman (who became the countess); university students; a German doctor.

Two descriptions from Givner's biography will show the details Porter provided in the letter to Gordon. About the ship's doctor who became one of her most sympathetic characters she wrote:

The ship's doctor is an old Heidelberg student with a grand hooked nose, a fine head, and two sabre scars across his cheek and forehead. He walks like an officer, and stands at attention apparently, for half an hour at a time, gazing at the water with the kindest, most serviceable pair of tan eyes you can imagine: they are almost maternally sweet and good. I went to him for help, having broken out with that dangerous tropical disease known as heat rash. All over I was a welter. He gave me a lotion he had mixed for himself, being, he said, a martyr to heat rash. It worked like a charm. Was there anything else he could do for me? No, I was in perfect health otherwise. "You do not look like a tough voman," he told me, "but it is possible you are very strong inside," and he tapped the front of his tunic. I said I thought I was fairly tough inside. . . . He himself has a bad heart, and may drop dead at any time.

La Condesa in the novel was based on Porter's sketch of a fifty-year-old once beautiful Cuban woman who had been active in the Cuban revolution and was being exiled. Her mind was unhinged, and she carried on long conversations with passengers, often talking about her husband who had been killed fighting in the revolutionary movement in Cuba, and speaking of her sons who were in hiding. Porter believed the woman had not been married and did not have sons, that Cuba was her martyred husband, and the revolutionary students her sons. Porter quoted the Cuban woman as saying: "My sons were students who defied the government, and they were right. Youth must defy governments, even though it means persecution, exile, death. The young must not throw away their beautiful lives being stupid and living like half-dead things—leave that for an old woman."[4] Porter made many changes in the sketch, incorporating into the fictional La Condesa some of her own characteristics—her infatuation with young men and her fading beauty. The character sketches and incidents described in the letter do not indicate that Porter was then acutely aware of the rise of the Nazi spirit. The political overtones of the novel are not to be found in the letter.

Porter also used, in fictional form, other people and events from her past. There is reason to believe that Hart Crane, one of her acquaintances in Mexico not long before his suicide, is portrayed in the novel. Porter seems to have apportioned certain of Crane's characteristics among three of her fictional men: the boorish Denny; Echegaray, the woodcarver who is deprived of his means to express himself artistically when his knife is taken from him; and Baumgartner, the alcoholic lawyer who threatens suicide by jumping from the ship.

Crane excitedly wrote friends on 30 March 1931 that he would soon sail for Mexico where he would establish himself in the country after spending a week with his "old and wonderful friend, Katherine Anne Porter."[5] During the voyage, Crane spent hours talking to Dr. Hans Zinsser, the Harvard bacteriologist then on his way to Mexico with "a half dozen rats in the hold loaded with the deadly typhus."[6]

The night the ship sailed from Havana, Crane had been drinking heavily, and he came upon the bacteriologist who was dropping overboard a parcel wrapped in paper. The package broke open when it hit the water, and Crane saw two white rats struggling in the water and knew they were the typhus-infected specimens Dr. Zinsser was taking to Mexico for his experiments. Crane was, Philip Horton says, "seized by the drunken fantasy that his friend was diabolically poisoning the harbor of Havana, and began to shout frenzied warnings of the danger at the top of his voice."[7] Dr. Zinsser in *As I Remember Him* says that Crane spoke as if "scanning lines from his Bridge poem":—

> The Doctor has thrown rats into the harbor of Havana.
> The Doctor has thrown typhus rats into the water.
> There will be typhus in Havana.
> The Doctor has thrown rats into the harbor.[8]

Crane finally had to be confined to his cabin for the night. Porter must have known of this rat incident, either from hearing about it from Crane or from reading Horton's biography of Crane, which appeared in 1937 and for which she had provided a long account of her relations with Crane.

The scene in *Ship of Fools* describing the drowning of Echegaray while rescuing the fat bulldog Bébé, deliberately thrown overboard by Ric and Rac, may well be indebted to Crane's observing Dr. Zinsser casting the rats overboard. The drunken Denny, who has been stalking the prostitute Pastora, sees a "long dark bundle"— almost the same expression used by Horton—strike the water. Then Ric and Rac run by, and Denny is aware of another bundle hitting the water, followed by cries from steerage. Greatly agitated, he begins to cry, and in his drunkenness he is almost as emotional as Crane seeing the rats in the water.

Other characteristics of Crane are seemingly transferred to Echegaray, the Jesus-like Basque (even his nationality reminds one of Crane, who wore a Basque jersey). From bits of wood in his bundle Echegaray carves small animals to sell to first-class passengers. After his knife—and thus his hope—is taken from him, he sits crying, just as Crane, his artistic powers declining, often cried. Porter leaves Echegaray a shadowy figure, and she provides multiple reasons to explain his rescue of Bébé: that it is a completely disinterested act; or, as the priest thinks, "a blamable disregard for his life"; or the hope of reward or a hero's welcome; or a longing for death—suicide without the stigma associated with self-destruction. These multiple choices proposed by various characters in the novel parallel fairly closely the speculations on the causes and meaning of Crane's suicide: his disavowal of a world gone mad; his psychic, sexual malaise; his attempt to find mystical union with the universe.[9]

Crane joined Porter in Mixcoac, a Mexico City suburb, but she and her lover Pressly (who was distressed by Crane's homosexual activities) soon regretted inviting him to be a house guest. Horton reports, "Crane, caught in the quickening constrictions of his fate . . . was fast becoming an insupportable companion."[10] When Porter and Pressly reached the end of their endurance, Horton says, they "persuaded [Crane] to find a home of his own, [and] he rented the adjoining building, which, unfortunately for her, was vacant."[11] This first rupture in the friendship of the two writers was apparently a distressing one. Crane had been put in jail on 24 April, and he soon afterwards was troubled with a painful rash, perhaps caused by unsanitary conditions in the jail. After a restless night, he sent this message to Porter on 28 April: "HAVE GONE TO THE MANCERA [a local hotel] UNTIL THE FIRST. EXCUSE MY WAKEFULNESS PLEASE. P. S. NO. HAVEN'T BEEN BUSY WITH 'LOVERS.' JUST YEOWLS AND FLEAS. LYSOL ISN'T NECESSARY IN THE BATHTUB. HAVEN'T GOT 'ANYTHING' YET.[12] This angry postscript is echoed in *Ship of Fools*: Denny's cabin mate David, who is Jenny's lover, is a fanatic about germs and constantly cleans the wash basin with something Denny thinks is carbolic acid. David is outraged to see Denny take a sponge bath, leaving his body hair sticking to the side of the lavatory, and David vows to wash the bowl with disinfectant as soon as the Texan leaves the room. In an earlier printed version of this episode, which appeared in *Harper's Magazine* of November 1950, Porter used the word *lysol*.

After Crane wrote abject notes begging forgiveness, the two writers again went on seeing each other. Horton indicates that Crane's midnight brawls with his homosexual partners continued, but that it was not the violence or Crane's sordid sexual adventures that disturbed Porter; it was rather "the terrible spectacle of a great talent, an essentially noble spirit, caught in the grip of a slow, inexorable disintegration."[13]

The final break was, for Crane, unexpected. In a long letter of explanation and self-justification, Crane told Lorna Dietz that he found Porter's disposition quite different from what it was in New York. He admitted that he said outrageous things to her when he was drunk, but everything had been going smoothly until he invited her to dinner. He made extensive preparations for the meal, liberally sampling the tequila all along, but Porter did not come to dinner. Crane roared into town, drank more, and later that night quarreled with Porter at her gate. He recalled saying to her: " 'Katherine Anne, I have my opinion of you.' I was furious, of course, and I still have no reason for doubting that [Eugene Pressly] simply devised that insult deliberately."[14] Crane did not see Porter again, and she did not answer his letter of apology.

In her own carefully controlled recollections of this event, Porter did not mention the missed dinner party, but she did describe the scene at the gate: Crane called her to pay his taxi fare (she said he claimed never to remember events when he was drunk but always sent money around the next day for the taxi fare) and he wanted to come in, but she was "tired to death" and "at the end" of her patience and told him to go home. She continued: "It was then that he broke into the monotonous obsessed dull obscenity which was the only language he knew after reaching a certain point of drunkenness, but this time he cursed . . . the moon, and its light: the heliotrope, the heaven-tree, the sweet-by-night, the star jessamine, and their perfumes. He cursed the air we breathed together. . . .

But those were not the things he hated. He did not even hate us, for we were nothing to him. He hated and feared himself."[15]

In the novel Denny, the Texan, endowed with many of Crane's boisterous, vulgar characteristics, is brutally assaulted by Mrs. Treadwell on the night of the dinner given by the Spanish dancers. Denny, after trailing the prostitute Pastora for days, hoping to avail himself of her services free or cheaply, is determined to have her that night. Drunkenly stumbling after her, he mistakenly stops in front of Mrs. Treadwell's door (an approximation of Porter's gate), yelling out "thick-tongued descriptions of the Gothic excesses he intended to commit upon Pastora's person, of which rape would be the merest preliminary" (*Ship of Fools* 464). Mrs. Treadwell (somewhat tipsy herself) has just painted on a face something like Pastora's; her assumed face seems to reveal "something sinister in the depths of her character" (462). When she flings open the door, Denny grabs her, saying, "Come out here, you whore" (464). She tells him he has made a mistake, but he is too drunk to see that her painted face is merely a mask. She knocks him to the floor, strikes him with her fist, and then pounds his face with the sharp heel of her shoe. When she learns the next morning that the story is out that Pastora attacked Denny with an ice pick, she laughs with great pleasure. She makes no attempt to make amends to her victim; and, as is fitting for such a self-isolated character, when leaving the ship at Gijón in the boat that carries the passengers to shore, she sits with her back toward the *Vera,* facing away from truth.

Although Porter made changes in the actual events at the gate in order to fit the incident into her fictional narrative, the scenes are remarkably similar, with a vivid addition—Mrs. Treadwell's violent retribution against the errant, vulgar, brutal male, a vengeance taken significantly only when her character is masked.

Porter also incorporates some of Crane's moods into her characterization of Herr Baumgartner, who had failed as a lawyer because of excessive drinking. On his tenth wedding anniversary, he quarrels with his wife and threatens to jump from the ship. His wife's reaction is similar to Porter's nonchalance when Crane once threatened to jump from the roof: "Oh don't," Porter said, "It's not high enough and you'll only hurt yourself." Crane laughed and came down.[16] "Yes," Frau Baumgartner says to her husband, "you will make a big disturbance and be rescued like Bébé." When her husband points

out that the Basque had drowned, she replies, "You make me sick!"
(453–54).

As he stands at the rail considering jumping, Herr Baumgartner,
in his self-pity, blames Mrs. Treadwell, then passing by, for her
indifference to his suffering. Actually, after she passes him and he
"turned a face of despair towards them, almost an appeal for help"
(459–60), Mrs. Treadwell says to her companion, "He seems awfully
sick somehow, perhaps dying" (460). His malaise, annoying though
it is to those about him, is fully as acute as Crane's.

These three fictional characters are not Crane—they have been
given some of Crane's characteristics or they perform acts that Porter
connected with Crane. (Givner suggests that Porter also used characteristics of her hated first husband in her portrayal of Denny.)
The Crane affair, unpleasant as it must have been for Porter, had
time to enter her subconscious mind, to be transformed into art in
a process she describes: "Now and again thousands of memories
converge, harmonize, arrange themselves around a . . . coherent
form, and I write a story."[17]

In *Ship of Fools* Porter expresses—if the foregoing speculations be
correct—a sharply ambivalent attitude toward the poet. Jenny, one
of Porter's major spokeswomen, says on the morning of Echegaray's
funeral: "Just think of him being left there all by himself" (324).
But at the funeral, Jenny thinks the whole scene "unreal, a pan-
tomime[;] . . . there was nothing that had ever been alive in that
dark swaddle of canvas; and even as she wondered at her callousness,
she felt her eyes filling with perfectly meaningless tears, tears for
nothing at all, that would change nothing, that would not even
ease the pain of her emptiness; and through a mist she saw the
canvas leap outward and strike the water" (328).

The Novel

In 1932, with her voyage to Europe still clearly in mind, Porter
read Sebastian Brant's *Das Narrenschiff* (1494). As she began planning her own novel, she says in the prefatory note, she took from
Brant's work the idea of "this simple almost universal image of the
ship of this world on its voyage to eternity." Brant's influence on
the novel is much more pronounced than most critics have seen.

Edwin H. Zeydel wrote of Brant: "Brant was a man of deep

religious convictions and of stern morality, even to the point of prudishness. His motives were of the highest. He wanted to elevate his generation, and dreamed too of improving its political condition through moral regeneration. . . . Yet he was also nervous and irritable, positive and dogmatic, a carping satirist of the very follies of which he himself may often have been guilty. His tendency to seek weaknesses and flaws in others was congenital. His morality was philistine."[18] Brant satirized the foibles and weaknesses of his fellows, but as Henry Charles Lea wrote in the *Cambridge Modern History*, "the important feature of the work is the deep moral earnestness which pervades its jest and satire; man is exhorted never to lose sight of his salvation, and the future life is represented as the goal to which his efforts are to be directed."[19] Porter, while adopting much of Brant's moral earnestness and his satiric thrusts, made special use not only of his ship imagery but of his deadly sins as well: sins against society including injustice, dishonesty, and uncharitableness; sins of the church and the clergy, such as ill-advised prayers, irreverence in church, clerical excesses; sins of lawyers, doctors, patients, women of ill repute, beggars; sins at the carnival—to name only some of Brant's categories—are also abundant on Porter's ship. Unlike Brant, however, Porter presented developed characters, not abstractions.

The allegory of good and evil is implicit in Porter's work, but she made her meaning clear by using as a focal point the rise of fascism in the 1930s, and the worldwide calamity that resulted from the mass movements led by Hitler, Mussolini, and Franco. She catalogued in detail the inertia and political naiveté among most of the Americans and Europeans on the *Vera*: the anti-Negro, anti-Mexican sentiments of the Texan Denny, attitudes still prevalent long after nazism and fascism were officially dispelled in Germany and Italy; the Spanish dancers, prostitutes, pimps, criminals, who manage to terrify the whole ship and to survive and even thrive while doing so; the Fatherland consciousness, pigheadedness, anti-Semitism, self-pity, and cruelty of the Germans—observations based on Porter's personal experiences on the ship bound for Europe in 1931 and in Germany itself, observations she confirmed or revised in light of later developments in Germany. Porter incorporated virtually all of Brant's fools into her political pararble.

One of Porter's most skillful accomplishments in the novel is her deft handling of point of view, which constantly shifts from character to character. As readers we see characters and events from multiple angles of vision, and we begin to understand the complexity of their interweaving. No one observer has the "truth"; no one observer speaks for Porter. Mrs. Treadwell's bruised arm, for example, results, as the reader knows, from a beggar's pinch; but, when Dr. Schumann sees it, he immediately concludes it was caused by an amorous lover. Time and again, interpretations that seem logical to those making the judgments are proved wrong.

The opening section describing the embarkation, with the rubric Baudelaire's "Quand partons-nous vers le bonheur?" (When shall we set out toward happiness?) used ironically, is a sustained mood piece, a nearly perfect introduction to the action and events that follow. Veracruz is described with impressively realistic details, and by implication Porter extends her Veracruz to represent all commercial cities and her passengers all the people of the world. Veracruz is a "little purgatory between land and sea," and the reader soon learns that the embarking passengers are to leave one purgatory for another on board ship, and for yet another at their port of destination. At first, the sights and sounds, the local color, are stronger than the passengers themselves. The capitalist-proletariat leitmotif that runs through the novel is introduced early: the Mexican capitalists are bloodthirsty, unfeeling, confident they will last a while longer; the proletariat are innocent victims (as is the boy killed in the bungled bombing), exploited and mistreated, as are the hundreds of Spaniards in steerage. Class and social differences are evident throughout the novel, not only between first class and steerage, but in first class itself, with its own bitter divisions.

One of the most horror-provoking bits of realism, the maimed beggar, is found in Brant. As Zeydel in his translation of *The Ship of Fools* rendered the passage:

> To beg some men will always choose,
> Though they could work if but they would,
> They're young and strong, their health is good,
> Save that their back they'll not incline,
> These sluggards have a corpse's spine.
> Their children in their youth they train
> To profit well by beggar's gain,
> To learn the cries—a mumper's token—,
> Or else they'd have their bones all broken

> Or so be maimed with welt and bruise
> That they would scream from sheer abuse.

In Porter's version, the beggar, who had been deformed by a master beggar, appears on the terrace in Veracruz every morning (just as the clowns and dwarfs in "The Circus" appear in the circus tent every day). Partially blind, and dumb, he crawls along the sidewalk like a dog, "wagging his hideous shock head from side to side slowly in unbearable suffering. The men at the table glanced at him as if he were a dog too repulsive even to kick" (4–5). Porter uses, as she often did, animal imagery to describe humans; but, in this instance, we see an example of her concreteness as opposed to Brant's abstraction, and her version of the perfidy of beggars surpasses Brant in horror, setting, and tone.

The travelers straggle into the plaza and the restaurant slowly, and the reader sees them as the travelers themselves would view a group awaiting passage. The Mexican waiters stare insolently at the motley assortment, including the fat couple with the fat bulldog Bébé. The night before, the clerk had told the woman, "No, Señora, even if this is only Mexico still we do not allow dogs in our rooms" (12). The humor and gentle irony of this passage is followed by a comic, mock-heroic description: "The ridiculous woman had kissed the beast on his wet nose before turning him over to the boy who tied him up in the kitchen patio for the night. Bébé the bulldog had borne his ordeal with the mournful silence of his heroic breed, and held no grudges against anybody" (12). Porter's control of language is beautifully demonstrated here. Her difficult personal life is reflected in this scene, also. Her youngest sister, called "Baby," was enamored of her pet bulldog, saying she loved it more than anything else. Givner points out that in 1936 Porter was "appalled" by her sister's kissing the dog. She was seldom on cordial terms with her sister, finally breaking with her entirely, and many years later she used the dog and her sister in the novel.

The horror of the death of the young Indian boy, killed by mistake in the bombing of the Swedish Embassy, makes almost no impression on the travelers, and they are equally unconcerned about the Indian arrested by the police. Herr Rieber predicts the man will be shot, but his pre-Nazi mentality is not to be trusted—he wants all inferior races shot or put into gas ovens. The bored reactions of the Mexicans discussing the bombing become a parable for human indifference to violence and symbolic of the madness for which the world was headed in less than ten years.

Porter at first gives only surface impressions of the Germans, Americans, the Swede, the three Swiss, the Spanish dancers, and their two children, but slowly a few of the travelers begin to appear in focus: the Huttens, "parents" of Bébé, and Mrs. Treadwell, with a large bruise on her arm. In describing Mrs. Treadwell, Porter emphasizes not only the beastliness of the beggar woman who pinches her in anger but also the aloofness and alienation shown by Mrs. Treadwell in refusing to give alms to the beggar. In groups, couples, and one by one, Porter introduces her cast of characters, and we see many of them again through the eyes of the ship's medical officer, Dr. Schumann. From his first description, the doctor seems suspiciously flawed—he has two dueling scars on his face—but the reader's reaction of repulsion at the scarred face is misguided and proved wrong. Dr. Schumann is not a bigoted fraternity man, but a professional man of talent, a trustworthy observer with a clinical eye and human compassion. He is representative of what was good in a Germany of the past, but he is dying of heart disease, just as the "good" Germany is dying.

The doctor soon wanders away, and a Mexican bride and groom become the center of attention. They are almost totally shrouded during the whole trip, and they, with the Mexican woman, baby, and maid, all virtually completely outside the action of the novel, seem less fools than the other passengers. The fat Mexican in the cherry-colored shirt, a figure remarkably similar to Braggioni in "Flowering Judas," also seems shadowy at first, not menacing, faintly humorous, a mock revolutionary.

With their luggage in their cabins, the passengers begin to take on clearer identity. Love, sex, and jealousy are introduced in the first pairings on the *Vera*: the pre-Nazi, piglike Rieber and his Lizzi, Arne Hansen, a sex-ridden Swede, and Lizzi. The feud between the two men over Lizzi lasts the entire trip, coming to a climax the night of the captain's ball. The Spanish dancers, without their pimps, are ogled by Denny, the sex-crazed, perenially unsuccessful Texan. He shares a cabin with Herr Glocken and David Scott, lover of the American girl Jenny Brown, who caused a scandal in Veracruz by appearing in slacks. David and Jenny are constantly quarreling, consuming each other in their love-hate relationship. (This relationship closely parallels that of Porter and Pressly in 1931.)

Frau Rittersdorf, disappointed because she had not made a profitable marriage in Mexico, had in pique turned against dark-skinned races; to assure proper respect from her cabin mate, she had sent herself flowers, with appropriate messages, signing one with the name of a dead baron. The reader's initial contempt for this vain woman is tempered with her diary entry on Jenny and David. She finds the names musical but sentimental: "Jenny Angel—the real name is, I suppose, Jane, Johanna Engel it would be, and much better, in the German—and David Darling. The latter is a common surname as well as a usual term of affection among Americans, I believe; much less among the frozen English naturally, though it does seem to be a corruption of the word *Dear,* Dearling, the diminutive; this would sound as if pronounced Darling, since the English have a slovenly way of speaking certain words" (84). The entry is comic not only because Frau Rittersdorf has parodied, unconsciously, much German philological pedantry, but also because it is clear that Porter is not taking herself too seriously. It is well known that she kept a journal about the voyage (in the form of that long letter to Caroline Gordon), and in the novel she is, in effect, casting doubts on the pretensions of diary keepers and the validity of their observations.

The Huttens' fat bulldog Bébé is comic and ludicrous, a perfect illustration of Dr. Johnson's famous definition: "Bulldog . . . A dog of particular form, remarkable for his courage. He is used in baiting the bull; and his species is so peculiar to Britain, that they are said to degenerate when they are carried to other countries." Bébé has degenerated, but through no fault of his own. Overfed and overprotected, he is constantly seasick. He is one of Porter's few sympathetic characters on board the ship, and one feels pity for this degenerate bull-baiter who makes no protest when Ric and Rac toss him overboard.

Ric and Rac have been widely misinterpreted as pure incarnations of evil. Six-year-old twin children of Lola, one of the members of the Zarzuela company, their life is spent among whores and pimps. They are outcasts patterning their lives on a cartoon popular in Mexico that featured wirehaired terriers who "made fools of even the cleverest human beings in every situation, made life a raging curse for everyone near them, got their own way invariably by a wicked trick, and always escaped without a blow" (71). The twins outwit even their parents by throwing La Condesa's pearls overboard.

In some ways they seem, in their perversity and intransigence, outrageous caricatures of Porter's—and Everyman's—own characteristics as a child; more important, they have been shaped by the Zarzuela company and by the society that supported the newspaper cartoons. Porter did not set out—in the characters of Ric and Rac or in some of the pre-Franco Spaniards, pre-Nazi Germans, or bigoted southerners—to define the exact nature of good and evil. Nor does she see any possibility for human redemption. Echegaray, the Jesus-like character, sacrifices himself to rescue Bébé—a parody of Jesus' dying for humanity—but nobody understands, nobody cares, least of all the priests.

It is in "Part II, Kein Haus, Keine Heimat . . ." (No House, No Home), in which we see the travelers, alienated, without permanent house or home, revealing much of their true nature. Three women are of special interest; all three are, in one way or another, spokeswomen for Porter. Jenny, the young artist, seems partially autobiographical: she is from the South, from a large family that disapproved of her wanting to be an artist; she has been much interested in liberal causes and believes in direct participation in political protest. Unfortunately, Jenny has allowed David to influence her work, and in her paintings she no longer uses the bright colors she once favored. She is only slightly disillusioned; she is another Miranda still capable of seeing the world (if not always her lover) with perception. The love-hate relationship of Jenny and David is one of the major themes of the novel.

Mrs. Treadwell, the forty-five-to-forty-six-year-old divorcée, wants to withdraw from all contact with her fellow passengers but is inevitably drawn into the life of Freytag, the handsome businessman who both loves and hates his Jewish wife. Mrs. Treadwell, a heavy drinker, unwittingly reveals that Freytag's wife is Jewish, and she thus brings about his downfall among the Germans at the captain's table. She is, then, a traitor, just as Laura is a traitor in "Flowering Judas," and in her alienation, she is much like the unnamed narrator in "Hacienda." Her assault upon Denny comes at the end of the captain's dinner and is her vengeance taken upon the errant male.

La Condesa is also a spokesperson for Porter; a slightly grotesque, once beautiful woman constantly in need of sex, she accepts the company of the Cuban medical students. She is also in need of drugs, which she receives from Dr. Schumann. But, with all her foibles and large and small human failings, she is much more than a decayed member of the aristocracy. She is grief stricken, driven to the point of madness by the uncertainty of the fate of her imagined sons. Her emotions are larger than life; but, in a world of dislocation, her sufferings are understandable and telling. Too, she alone understands and does not condemn the incestuous relationship of Ric and Rac, a bond that horrifies the doctor and the young ship's officer. Lastly, she is capable of love; and the love affair with the doctor, though doomed, is one of the most admirable examples of love in the novel.

The Germans, products of an authoritarian culture, are authoritarian, autocratic, sentimental. Except for Herr Rieber and the captain, they are not in themselves vicious but they can be led to cruelty. Their willingness to send Freytag away from the captain's table because of his Jewish wife is presented as a parable of the rise of nazism and anti-Semitism. The pride in race, the self-satisfaction of the remaining Germans, the failure of the intellectual Dr. Schumann to defend Freytag—all are realistic and at the same time symbolic. Porter has extended her allegory to the universal human condition; she shows the racism of Denny and of Löwenthal. When the members of the Zarzuela company steal the prizes for the captain's gala, virtually everyone in the first class sees what they are doing, but nobody does anything about it.

Löwenthal, a Jew, has many of the despicable traits of the Germans. He is self-satisfied, a shrewd businessman selling religious goods and bragging of his work, just as Chaucer's Pardoner did. "There's money in it" (96), Löwenthal says; it has nothing at all to do with religion, it is just business.

One of the most pathetic of the Germans is Johann Graf, the handsome young boy taking his dying uncle to Germany for a last visit. The grotesque old uncle, a religious fanatic, thinks he has the power of healing, but he is too unobservant to see the problems of his nephew, who is sex-starved and has no money to pay Concha for sexual favors. She is attracted to him but insists that he buy her love, suggesting that the boy kill the old man to get the money. Johann's agony (he takes the money but does not kill the uncle) and his initiation into sexual activity are followed by attempts to be kind to the old man, attempts that fail because the boy is misunderstood just as Stephen is in "The Downward Path to Wisdom."

Also of special interest is the fate of the agitator in the red shirt. At the funeral service, he often belches loudly and makes "the sign of the Cross with his thumb on the end of his nose" (326). The devout in steerage, angered, fall upon him and strike him a strong blow to the head. The reactions to the attack are tellingly analyzed, from Jenny's impotent tears, to Hansen's cry "Kill your enemies, not your friends!" (328), to the captain's disgust, "Let them decimate each other if they like, but not on my ship" (344). When the revolutionist leaves the ship, he is dazed and has to be helped. Dr. Schumann thinks he will recover and get into more trouble, but the account is clearly a parable of the weakening of the revolutionary movement.

The huge cast of characters introduced in the first section is seen intimately and distantly, wrongly and obliquely in this long second section. The third section begins with a quotation from Saint Paul: "For here have we no continuing city. . . ." In the central scene at the captain's gala, the parallel to Brant is explicit: he wrote of the carnival fools, revelers who often pretend to mask their identity in order to commit immoral acts; at Porter's carnivallike dinner, all semblance of morality is swept away. Hiding behind a mask, Mrs. Treadwell attacks Denny; the thieving, amoral Spanish dancers propose, symbolically, a pact with Germany; Herr Baumgartner goose-steps and is followed by goose-stepping children—a modern Pied Piper leading the children to destruction; the pathetic Herr Glocken sports his pink necktie inscribed *"Girls, follow me!"* (419); Hansen attacks Herr Rieber. The last vestiges of civilized behavior are stripped away in the ribald Cucaracha song, in the drunkenness of David, Denny, Baumgartner, and Jenny, and in the dishonest drawing for prizes. One or two characters stop at the brink of this headlong plunge into barbarism. Johann, his sexual desire fulfilled, will not lie, will not say he loves Concha. The Mexican couple, in their happiness and naiveté, want to die young or live forever. The other passengers remain untouched by the madness of the night. The injured are treated; the gulled do nothing about their betrayal; Mrs. Treadwell turns her back on the events; David and Jenny go on quarreling; the Germans go on making their plans for reentering the Fatherland. The professor speaks for them the cliché, "At last we are nearing home, and we are, after all, all good Germans together. Let us thank God for his blessings" (493).

Harry J. Mooney, Jr., in *The Fiction and Criticism of Katherine Anne Porter,* argues that the novel is too restricted, that Porter portrays a hate-driven world "little susceptible to the claims of reason and intelligence." Mooney isolates what he thinks is a major defect of the novel: "the possibility of human nobility" is absent. One could argue, however, with equal validity, that had Porter emphasized "human nobility" or even the possibility of human nobility, she would not have given a true picture of the 1930s or of much human experience in the twentieth century. Porter sees the possibility offered by the wood-carver; but, because of the human condition, his act does not bring salvation, is not even a worthy example.

More recently, Darlene Harbour Unrue argues in *Truth and Vision in Katherine Anne Porter's Fiction* that Dr. Schumann and Jenny have made progress toward truth and thus the novel is not as pessimistic as some critics have asserted. She believes that the doctor has progressed farther than Jenny, for he has "made peace with death and has grasped the essential meaning of good and evil and love and hate." Jenny, Unrue argues, "will be receptive to [the] transforming power" of love "when she does find it because she is not burdened with false hopes in systems, patterns, and ideals."[20]

Porter has, by the end of the novel, explored attitudes toward life and death, love and sex, religion and religiosity, love and hate, racism and politics; she has presented the deadly sins in old forms and in new guises. She has drawn upon all her years of experience, all her artistic powers, and upon artistic methods she learned from Joyce, James, Eliot, Brant, and others.

The enormous sales of *Ship of Fools* and the income from film rights made Porter wealthy so that she could live the elegant life she always imagined for herself, but the novel did little for her literary reputation. Although her supporters still praise the work, it is no longer read as widely as her short stories and short novels. It is, however, a gigantic work, subtle and forceful, naturalistic and symbolic, still a powerful moral and political allegory.

Chapter Six
The Essays and Occasional Writings

Porter's essays and reviews are much more difficult to evaluate than her fiction. As she explained in the foreword to *The Days Before,* her essays and reviews—unlike the fiction—were requested by publishers who set space and subject limitations. She insisted that although she often wrote under great pressure, she always expressed her ideas as clearly as possible and regarded the articles that she chose to reprint as an accurate journal of her "thinking and feeling." The articles were avowedly written for money but they were not "the other half of a double life. . . . The two ways of working helped and supported each other: I needed both."[1]

Porter herself made the selections for *The Days Before* (1952), but the pieces for *The Collected Essays and Occasional Writings* (1970) were assembled by several of her friends at a time when she was ill. Porter was not grateful for their help; she was outraged at their presumption. It is true that too many ephemeral pieces are included, but it is far from certain that Porter, by then in failing health, would have been more judicious in her own selections. It is clear from a reading of the large collection that many of her articles and reviews were written hastily and some are in a style quite inferior to her usual standards. Her important critical essays are discussed under the headings used in the 1970 volume. Emphasis is placed on pieces that illuminate her critical positions and her own creative works.[2]

Critical

The collection's lead article, "On a Criticism of Thomas Hardy" (1940), is an effective beginning essay in which Porter brandished her biting and heavy satire in deprecating Hardy's critics. She aims her heaviest salvoes against T. S. Eliot, who after his conversion, she asserts, was writing literary judgments that "assumed the tone of lay sermons." Porter proceeds to quote from Eliot's attack on

Hardy and then craftily and wittily demolishes his arguments. Her defense of the novelist and her iconoclastic attack on the pontifications of the poet are sustained throughout the essay. In her role as Eliot-slayer Porter is remarkably effective but not entirely fair. Many years later, in a letter to a cousin published as "On First Meeting T. S. Eliot," her attitude toward the poet had changed completely, and she called him a genius.

Porter was never a wholehearted admirer of D. H. Lawrence, and her views toward him continued to harden over the years. In 1959 she published "A Wreath for the Gamekeeper," a slashing attack against Lawrence and *Lady Chatterley's Lover*: "Why should I defend a worthless book just because it has a few dirty words in it? Let it disappear of itself and the sooner the better." Porter found Lawrence to be a badly flawed artist who either did not know what he was doing, or, if he did, was pretending to be doing something else. She sums up the theme of the novel as nothing more than "the activities of the rutting season between two rather dull persons." She does not object to Lawrence's obscenity but to "his misuse and perversions of obscenity, his wrong-headed denial of its true nature and meaning. Instead of writing straight, healthy obscenity, he makes it sickly sentimental, embarrassingly so. . . . I object to this pious attempt to purify and canonize obscenity, to castrate the Roaring Boy, to take the low comedy out of sex." Like her grandmother, Porter held strong opinions and was more than willing to express them. Her article is beautifully written, but again, as with her criticism of Eliot, she is unfair to Lawrence. Taking an even-handed approach to a literary work was not one of Porter's virtues as a critic. Instead, her personal biases, her moods of the moment, controlled her critical stances.

When Porter was in a good mood, when she liked a writer, she could and often did write sensitively and effectively. "Reflections on Willa Cather" (1952) is a delicately phrased appreciation of a major American writer, one who influenced Porter extensively. The essay is particularly important because Porter explains not only what Cather meant to her but also some of her own background reading in twentieth-century literature. When Porter began to read Cather, she also read James, Yeats, Conrad, Joyce, and Stein (Stein's *Tender Buttons* was, she felt, symptomatic of much modern literature, which hid lack of feeling behind "disordered syntax" or "tricky techniques.") After savoring the new literature and art and music, Porter saw, finally, that her own artistic views were more akin to those of Cather. The essay tells us as much about Porter as it does about Cather, and is, above all, a ringing defense of the provincial in literature: "all true art is provincial . . . [it is] of the very time and place of its making, out of human beings who are . . . particularly limited by their situation, . . . whose lives begin each one at an individual unique center."

"It is Hard to Stand in the Middle" (1950) is a well-reasoned, artistic defense of Ezra Pound. Porter acknowledges James, Joyce, Yeats, Eliot, and Pound as writers who were important to her as she developed her own talent: "The beginning artist is educated by whoever helps him to learn how to work his own vein, who helps him to fix his standards, and who gives him courage." Porter rightly emphasizes Pound's incessant labors for other writers, but she also sees that he was opinionated, that he had a gift for making enemies as well as friends, qualities she perhaps recognized as also her own, though she did not openly admit to them. She sees that Pound was not only anti-Semitic (as she herself was, though never openly, as he was) but also anti-Christian, and she notes (never indicating that she is describing, to a lesser degree, herself) that when Pound ventured beyond art and poetry, he was liable to commit the grossest mistakes. Nevertheless, she sees him "as one of the great poets of his time," whose advice to young poets "was unfathomably good and right," and she concludes optimistically that "fighting the dark" would "survive and live again largely because of his life and example."

"The Art of Katherine Mansfield" (1937) is an all-too-brief comment on Mansfield's best stories. The essay is slighter than the one on Pound, for example, and seemingly only partially because of space limitations. Porter admired Mansfield but she says she hated Mansfield's "slimy crowd of friends."[3] She feels that Mansfield's reputation and prestige as a writer were deserved, but she cannot ignore Mansfield's "personal life of constant flight and search." She relegates Mansfield to "that ghostly company of unfulfilled, unhappy English artists who died and are buried in strange lands." The appreciation lacks flair and the usual Porter grace and style.

"Orpheus in Purgatory" (1950), a brief, impressionistic essay on Rilke, is interesting gossip, but the book review editor apparently did not allow Porter scope to present Rilke more completely, and the essay is disappointing. "The Laughing Heat of the Sun" (1949), an appreciation of Edith Sitwell's work, is also slight. Porter writes

that Sitwell's work was that "of a deft artificer, and a most orna-
mental rose, meant to amuse and charm, never intended to be
mistaken for a natural flower." "On Christopher Sykes" (1951) has
several comic lines but is far too glib in its assessment of English
writers, past and present.

In "Virginia Woolf" (1950) Porter speaks of Woolf as "one of
the writers who touched the real life of my mind and feeling very
deeply; I had from that book [*The Voyage Out*] the same sense of
some mysterious revelation of truth I had got in earliest youth from
Laurence Sterne." Porter considers Woolf's every line of fiction or
criticism as lastingly valuable, that she was a "native" of the "ter-
ritory" of the arts, ranging freely in her homeland and "speaking
her mother tongue fearlessly."

Porter's "E. M. Forster" (1951) begins with a personal reminis-
cence and ends with an appreciation of his "admirable style." Since
she is known as a stylist herself, her comment is of special interest:
"his own style [is] spare, unportentous but serious . . . fearless
but not aggressive." She admires his *Two Cheers for Democracy*, which
was "an extension and enlargement of his thought, a record of the
life and feelings of an artist who has been in himself an example of
all he has defended from the first: the arts as a civilizing force,
civilization itself as the true right aim of the human spirit," and
she writes approvingly of his belief in the importance of love "not
in the mass, not between nations . . . but between one person and
another."

The last four essays in the section lack substance. Porter had
nothing important to say about Max Beerbohm's *And Even Now* or
Eleanor Clark's *Rome and a Villa*. She liked Lodwick Hartley's biography of Laurence Sterne but could not resist several supercilious
comments about the biographer. As she grew older she became more
garrulous, more dogmatic: in her essay "On Modern Fiction" (1965)
she explained her then current likes and dislikes in fiction, but her
assertions were unsupported and often out of focus.

Personal and Particular

"St. Augustine and the Bullfight" (1955) is one of Porter's most
interesting and revealing late essays. She moved among the lost
generation in Mexico during the 1920s, and in this piece she takes
as her controlling image Saint Augustine's Alypius who, though he

did not want to witness the combats of the gladiators, was nevertheless caught up in the gory sport, becoming more bloodthirsty
than any of his friends. Against that figure she places Katherine
Anne Porter, a young woman sympathetic to the Mexican revolution
but running with a pack of titled expatriates in Mexico. It was one
of the poet Shelley's great-great nephews who introduced a reluctant
Porter to the sport of bullfighting, and she describes the events,
the sights, the emotions with the style of James and the vividness
of Hemingway. She, too, became an aficionado, drawn in fascination
to the spectacle of death in the ring. The essay would have been an
excellent chapter in her autobiography (which was never written),
or it could easily have been converted into fiction. As it is, it stands
as one of her meaningful fragments, part of an unwritten life story
verging toward fiction, with Katherine Anne, not Miranda, its
central character.

"A Little Incident in the Rue de l'Odéon" (1964) is a sad tale.
Hemingway and Porter were in the bookshop, Shakespeare and
Company, in 1934 and were introduced by the proprietor Sylvia
Beach: "I want the two best modern American writers to know each
other!" The two egotists looked at each other, and Hemingway
departed. No words were spoken. Porter's analysis: "it must have
been galling to this most famous young man to have his name
pronounced in the same breath as writer with someone he had never
heard of, and a woman at that." Whatever the reason for Hemingway's action, Porter had her anecdote, and she was the heroine of
it.

Porter refers to the Hemingway incident in "A Letter to Sylvia
Beach" (1956). She mentions the meeting but does not dramatize
it, and she is not the heroine in this version: "I have never seen
him since. I am sure we have not been avoiding each other, it was
just no doubt the right thing to happen." Both writers were highly
competitive, and it is doubtful that they ever would have had anything meaningful to say to one another.

"Letters to a Nephew" (1948–63) are an embarrassment. Porter
pontificating on sacred and profane love to her nephew, then an
adult, is unintentionally comic, as she inadvertently casts herself in
a role more ridiculous than profound.

Porter's views on Dylan Thomas need to be seen in light of an
anecdote. Thomas met Porter at a New York party in 1950. He
was attracted to her, made drunken approaches, and offered to take

her home. When she refused his offer and prepared to leave, he picked her up and held her toward the ceiling until John Malcolm Brinnin intervened. The incident was the stuff of literary gossip: it was reported in detail in Brinnin's *Dylan Thomas in America,* it was dramatized in Sidney Michaels' *Dylan,* and it was mentioned in Karl Shapiro's "Emily Dickinson and Katherine Anne Porter." Porter reviewed three books about Thomas (*Dylan Thomas in America, Leftover Life to Kill,* and *Dylan Thomas: Letters to Vernon Watkins*), without ever referring directly to that incident, though it undoubtedly influenced her view of the drunken, self-destructive poet. In the reviews she was fair, even generous to him, considering his great personal and financial problems; perhaps she was sympathetic because of the personal and financial problems she endured before her great financial success with *Ship of Fools.*

In "A Defence of Circe," originally published in *Mademoiselle* in 1954, Porter presents her own inimitable case for feminism. Circe, she argues, was not a witch, did not turn men into swine; instead, Circe's food and wine alowed men to reveal themselves as swine: "The delicate-minded goddess touched them then with her wand, the wand of the transforming truth, and penned the groaning, grunting, weeping, bewildered creatures in the sty back of the hall." Like Aunt Cat, a hater of weak men, Porter believed that women were strong and men piggish, and she created several literary figures in this mold: Braggioni in "Flowering Judas," the husband in "Rope," Denny in *Ship of Fools,* and many others—swines all.

The next three essays—"Pull Dick, Pull Devil," "The Flower of Flowers," and "A Note on Pierre-Joseph Redoute"—are among Porter's weakest writings, adding nothing of value to her critical reputation.

"Portrait: Old South" (1944), however, is one of her most important essays, for it shows us how she wished to remember her grandmother. As Porter wrote Katherine Sexton in 1960: "the Grandmother in my fiction is based on my own (Paternal) grandmother." In this essay Porter continues to fantasize about her family, but the truth is near the surface. She contrasts the lavish wedding party of her grandparents (possibly exaggerated) and the poverty of the family after the Civil War. She shows her grandmother coping with poverty and adversity, a skillful cook, a willful, forceful woman. The reality of life in Aunt Cat's cramped house is only hinted at, and Aunt Cat's sternness, her willingness to use corporal punishment, are treated with understanding, not resentment: "She never punished anyone until she was exasperated beyond all endurance, when she was apt to let fly with a lightning, long-armed slap at the most unexpected moments, usually quite unjustly and ineffectually." Porter's essay is helpful in understanding both Aunt Cat and the fictional grandmother.

"Audubon's Happy Land" (1939) is a description of a tour of plantation homes near St. Francisville, Louisiana. The essay is not quite social history, not quite local color, and the nostalgia for the Old South is somehow not quite in focus. Equally inconsequential are "A House of My Own" (1941) and "A Letter to the Editor of *The Village Voice*" (1956).

"The Necessary Enemy" (1948) begins frivolously but works toward personal revelations as Porter allied herself with Hawthorne's view of human nature: we do not "acknowledge the evils in ourselves" and "we also desire to be unhappy." She believed that "we create our own sufferings; and out of these sufferings we salvage our fragments of happiness."

In "Marriage Is Belonging" (1951) Porter wrote abstractly about a subject she knew intimately. The essay fails to hold the interest of the reader, and the same can be said of her patriotic piece "Act of Faith: 4 July 1942."

"The Future Is Now" (1950), however, is a more important statement on how to live in the shadow of the atomic bomb, how to avoid despair. Porter concludes midway between optimism and pessimism: "And yet it may be that what we have is a world not on the verge of flying apart, but an uncreated one—still in shapeless fragments waiting to be put together properly." She argues that if dropping the bomb was immoral, then making it was, too: the first criminal "then was the man who first struck fire from flint, for from that moment we have been coming steadily to this day and this weapon and this use of it. What would you have advised instead? That the human race should have gone on sitting in caves gnawing raw meat and beating each other over the head with the bones?"

Several of the next essays touch on communism, and Porter's attitude toward it changed drastically over the years; at times she adopted a condemnatory tone (in a 1947 letter to the *Nation*), and at other times, as in "On Communism in Hollywood" (1947), she treated anti-Communists satirically. She was generally not an adept political thinker, and her political statements—except for those about Mexico—can best be ignored, but her 1949 letter to the *Saturday Review of Literature* justifying her role in awarding the Bollingen-Library of Congress Award for Poetry to Ezra Pound is of great interest. In her letter, obviously defensive, she insists that she had voted for Pound according to the rules, that is, that the award should be given for the best volume of poetry pubilshed in 1948. In her view *The Pisan Cantos* was the best volume published that year, but she also thought that Pound was not at his best in this volume. She regrets that any award had been made at all, but she insists that she would vote the same way again. Her arguments justifying and defending her vote are not strongly convincing.

"Opening Speech at Paris Conference, 1952" is of importance because it is one of Porter's early public addresses and it contains her thoughts on artistic freedom. The contents of the other pieces at the end of this section—"Remarks on the Agenda" (1956), letters to the editor of *The Yale Review* (1961) and to the editor of the *Washington Post* (1959), and a "Speech of Acceptance" (1967) to the American Academy of Arts and Letters—are trivial.

Biographical

Porter considered Henry James a master and her essay on James appropriately goes far beyond an assessment of James as a writer; in it she makes both a personal and philosophical statement of her own approach to art. The conclusion to "The Days Before" (1943, revised 1952) is magnificently presented: "no man has ever seen any relations concluded. Maybe that is why art is so endlessly satisfactory: the artist can choose his relations, and 'draw, by a geometry of his own, the circle within which they shall happily *appear* to do so.' While accomplishing this, one has the illusion that destiny is not absolute, it can be arranged, temporized with, persuaded, a little here and there. And once the circle is truly drawn around its contents, it too becomes truth."

Porter wrote appreciatively of Ford Madox Ford (1942), not because each of his sixty books was good but because he made each work "as good as he was capable of making it at that moment" and because his life work and his vocation were the same. Poverty-stricken and neglected, Ford went on indomitably with his work, and Porter must have seen a parallel with her own career.

Porter was certainly not consistent in many of her literary assessments. Consider her changing views on Gertrude Stein. In "Everybody Is a Real One" (1927) Porter had her first say in print on Stein, and she was, if baffled at times, sympathetic, a young writer in the presence of one of the great influences of modern literature. One year later, like many another of Stein's readers, Porter had drawn away. In "Second Wind," she wrote a wicked and telling satire on Stein, mocking her mannerisms unmercifully. Porter then developed, years later, her third wind, also highly critical. There are speculations about why she mounted such a fierce attack on Stein.

Stein gave one explanation: In a 1945 letter she wrote that a young man called on her, sending in a note that his aunt was Katherine Anne Porter. Stein said "who is she, and he went quite white and said you know and I said no, and then he decided to take it as a joke, but it was a blow, he had evidently traveled far on his nephewship."

Was this incident perhaps the cause or partially the cause of Porter's slashing denunciation of Stein two years later? In "The Wooden Umbrella" (1947) Porter reviewed Stein's artistic and social careers and found both lacking, but she denied that the article was in response to her nephew's reception at Stein's apartment. In "Ole Woman River: A Correspondence with Katherine Anne Porter" (1966) she insisted to Donald Sutherland that she had written her attack on Stein before she knew about her nephew's interview with Stein. She had, she asserted, decided in the 1930s that Stein was "a little of a fraud."

Porter's attack on Stein in "The Wooden Umbrella" helped bring about the final break in the Porter-Herbst friendship. Herbst felt that Porter was attacking the entire modern movement in literature, a movement in which Porter had played a part, and she believed that Porter was moving toward the conservative literary majority. Herbst wrote Porter about the essay: "It reads so persuasively, but it isn't Stein." Herbst aggressively defended Stein in an article in the *Partisan Review*. The long friendship between these two strong-minded women was coming to an end, to be broken entirely a few years later by Herbst's reservations about *Ship of Fools*.[4]

"Eudora Welty and 'A Curtain of Green'" (1941) is a warm, enthusiastic appreciation. Without being pedantic, Porter sketched in essential facts from Welty's biography, her intellectual and artistic development, and the themes of her stories. Porter, the established artist, is not condescending in her introduction, and her comments are amazingly perceptive: she finds that Welty is not writing "false or labored" stories, that she is making a direct approach to her material, and that "there is even in the smallest story a sense of power in reserve which makes me believe firmly that, splendid beginning that this is, it is only the beginning."

The section ends with several occasional pieces requiring no comment: "A Sprig of Mint for Allen [Tate]" (1959), "On First Meeting T. S. Eliot" (1961), "Flannery O'Connor at Home" (1964), "From the Notebooks: Yeats, Joyce, Eliot, Pound" (1965), "Romany Marie, Joe Gould—Two Legends Come to Life" (1957), and "Jacqueline Kennedy" (1964).

Cotton Mather

Porter's biography of Cotton Mather, like the long-awaited *Ship of Fools,* was promised for decades. A few chapters did appear and they were included in her *Collected Essays,* but she was not a scholar nor did she have the scholarly temperament, and she was therefore ill-equipped to write a factual biography.

There were, however, several possible reasons Mather fascinated her. Joan Givner has speculated in her biography that Porter's interest in the New England puritan divine was an outgrowth of her Texas childhood, with its pervasive fundamentalist religious attitudes. The Mather biography may have been an attempt to exorcise that part of her past.[5]

Porter worked on the biography fitfully; it was, she said, like her knitting, to be picked up at odd moments. The published chapters are written with style and a wicked wit, but the facts are often wrong. Now that Kenneth Silverman has published his masterful *The Life and Times of Cotton Mather* (1984) we can see just how inaccurate Porter's biographical researches were. Her great gifts were, and remain, those of a fictionist, not a biographer or critic.

Mexican

The Mexican section of Porter's collected essays is of particular interest because it includes her excellent article "Why I Write About Mexico," which sheds light on her Mexican stories, and it brings together many fugitive pieces, including the introduction to her translation of Lizárdi's *The Itching Parrot* (1942), an elegantly written biographical and critical study, with keen insights into late eighteenth- and nineteenth-century Mexican life. Porter knew her Mexican history, and this sense of the Mexican past is reflected in the early Mexican stories. "Why I Write about Mexico" (1923) and "The Mexican Trinity" (1921) were discussed in Chapter 2; her other major writings on Mexico will be covered here.

In "Leaving the Petate" (1931), containing serious social criticism masked with a humorous account of Indian servants, Porter uses gentle humor to analyze the Mexican social revolution. She says of her maid, who with her marriage to a barber was putting aside the straw mat Indians usually slept on in exchange for a brass bed and respectability: "Her children will be added to the next generation of good little conservative right-minded dull people, like Enrique, or, with Eufemia's fighting spirit, they may become *mestizo* revolutionaries, and keep up the work of saving the Indian."

"The Fiesta of Guadalupe" (1923) is a vibrant description of the festivity, "which celebrates the initiation of Mexico into the mystic company of the Church, with a saint and a miracle all her own, not transplanted from Spain." Porter seems certain of her material in this piece, one of the first of her many excellent articles on Mexico.

"Where Presidents Have No Friends" (1922) contains Porter's analysis of the political situation in Mexico. She explores the failures and successes of the revolution and sees hope in the work of a few good people "in no wise connected with politics, . . . each in his own individual manner deeply concerned with the rebuilding of his country." Later, as in *Ship of Fools*, Porter took a bleak view of the chances for improvement, but in 1922 she believed, with Emerson and Thoreau, that individuals could make a difference.

"La Conquistadora" (1926) is a retelling of the story of Rosalie Evans, a Texas-born widow of an Englishman, who recaptured her Mexican hacienda after it had been seized during the Madero revolution. Evans had no understanding of the reasons for the Mexican revolution and she saw the history of the country only in terms of its economic effects upon herself. For over six years under almost continuous siege, she held her hacienda until finally she was ambushed and killed. Porter sees her fight as "gallant, brilliant and wholehearted, admirable as a mere exhibition of daring, energy and spirit," but Porter saw also that Evans fought to the death to prevent the Mexican people from realizing the very "foundation of their revolution." Porter's final judgment is clear and pointed: "As a human being she was avaricious, with an extraordinary hardness of heart and ruthlessness of will; and she died in a grotesque cause."

"Quetzalcoatl" (1926) is a review of D. H. Lawrence's *The Plumed Serpent*. Lawrence, she says, has risen above his usual confusion and with poetic power has found "a mystical truth." Though she praises the evocative powers of his language, she finds at the center of the rhetoric and sexual emotions "a sick void," and she concludes with a harsh but valid judgment: "When you have read this book read *Sons and Lovers* again. You will realize the catastrophe that has overtaken Lawrence."

"The Charmed Life" (1942) is an account of Porter's friendship with William Niven, the prototype of Givens in "María Concepción." His one interest in life was "digging up buried Indian cities," and his monomania made him appealingly unhuman, she says. The essay is evocative, but Porter does not portray him with any great depth of character; as a result, he seems more fragmentary than his fictional counterpart.

On Writing

"My First Speech," given to the American Women's Club in Paris in 1934, is important because it shows Porter thinking about her early life in terms of how she would later use it in her fiction: "I shall try to tell the truth, but the result will be fiction," she confesses. She believes that literary art needed, not types or imitators, but individuals, each with "something of his own to say" and with "his own language and style" in which to say it. The speech is not well organized, but it was probably effective when given a dramatic delivery.

"Notes on Writing" (1940) gives significant journal entries from Berlin in 1931 and 1932, from Basel in 1932, and Paris in 1936. The notes are forceful, and those made in Germany show Porter's awareness of some of the dangers in the rising nazism. These few entries make one wish for extensive publication of her journals. One other entry in particular is also provocative: she notes that she has thought of learning the parts of a harness and writing "them down in a note book. But to what end? I have two large cabinets full of notes already." The contents of those "two large cabinets" would be valuable for the insights they might provide.

In "1939: The Situation in American Writing," the first of "Three

Statements about Writing," Porter declares herself more "James-minded" than "Whitman-minded," and no one who reads her works will deny this obvious and beneficial influence. She questions whether either writer was more important in American literature than others such as Hawthorne, Melville, Stephen Crane, or Emily Dickinson, but she sagely advises young writers not to involve themselves in such literary scrimmaging.

More helpful is the second statement, a reprinting of the 1940 introduction to *Flowering Judas* in which she explains why she had not published more: "I was not one of those who could flourish in the conditions of the past two decades." She insists that her stories are fragments "of a much larger plan which I am still engaged in carrying out, and they are what I was then able to achieve in the way of order and form and statement in a period of grotesque dislocations in a whole society when the world was heaving in the sickness of a millennial change." Her statement is eloquent, but, though she often insisted that she had a master plan for her artistic work, alas, she never revealed it.

"Transplanted Writers" (1942), the third statement, is primarily interesting because in it she writes of the evil at work during World War II as "the oldest evil with a new name," and she agrees with E. M. Forster that only art and religion offer possibilities for creating order. She came to a similar conclusion in her essay on James, and much of her fiction, indeed, is an attempt to impose order on the chaos of human existence.

"No Plot, My Dear, No Story" (1942) is a satire on slick-magazine fiction and on writing schools that teach how to manipulate the "37 basic plots"; at the same time it is an extremely personal defense of serious short stories, which may or may not be commercial. Unfortunately, the satiric passages are more crude than Porter's usual style; and, since her examples are so obviously fictional, one almost forgets that she has in mind *The Saturday Evening Post, Mademoiselle,* and other "mass circulation" magazines.

In "On Writing" (1954), a recorded tape of a lecture at a writers' conference, Porter refers students to the great works of literature for instruction. She calls William Styron "a brilliant young writer," noting that there are "usually only one or two in a century."

In " 'Noon Wine': The Sources" (1956) Porter set out to trace the beginnings of characters, moods, and ideas that were finally transformed into her short novel. The essay is evocatively written and in many ways equal to one of James's prefaces, but we know from Givner's biography that Porter never admitted how deeply imbedded in her own childhood was that poverty-stricken world of her fiction. Indeed, as Givner shows, the Thompsons were relatives of the Porters and Harrison Porter once left his two youngest daughters with the Thompsons while he and Gay went to investigate a place to relocate. The Thompson house was cramped, Ellen Skaggs Thompson was an invalid, and her husband an easygoing man like the fictional Thompson. At the Thompson farm there was a hired man named Helton. Life at the Thompson farm was not far different from life at Aunt Cat's. These were Callie Porter's people, but she does not acknowledge them in the essay. Though the essay hides much of the truth about her past, in "Noon Wine" she confronts that past, recreating a world that in her nonfiction and interviews she obscured.

The Poetry

The *Collected Essays* ends with eight of Porter's poems. They are chiefly interesting for the light they shed on her life and her art. As Givner notes, Porter considered herself a "Sunday poet," but "poetry, like her early interest in the drama, imparted something valuable to her art, for it was from the poetic, lyrical grace of her prose that its quality derived."[6] Several of the poems illuminate Porter's life and emotions: "After a Long Journey," written to Gene Pressly from Berlin, is filled with a sense of despair about their relationship, which she later dealt with in the Jenny-David affair in *Ship of Fools*. "Measures for Song and Dance" is a seriocomic poem about Adam and Eve, Lilith and Adam, Lilith and Cain, and all of them together. It is comically concerned with good and evil, with sex, and with Porter's own version of feminism. Sunday poems have their place in the works of a fictionist, but it is a minor place.

A Christmas Story

Porter was deeply affected by the death in 1919 of her five-year-old niece, Mary Alice, Gay's daughter, and "A Christmas Story" is a tribute to that innocent, yet worldly-wise little girl. The slight memoir was originally published in *Mademoiselle* in 1958, and Delacorte Press brought out an edition, with illustrations by Ben Shahn, in 1967. There is no irony, no tension in the essay, and

Porter's golden memories of her young niece are not transformed into an artistic eulogy.

Sacco and Vanzetti

The Never-Ending Wrong (1977) was published five decades after the execution of Sacco and Vanzetti. In 1927 Porter went to Boston to demonstrate for the two anarchists, who were, she felt, caught in "a terrible miscarriage of justice." While she was in Boston protesting the imminent execution of the two, she made notes about her part in the protest, but she was not able at that time to shape her materials for publication. Toward the end of her life, aided by her companion William R. Wilkins, she worked again on her notes, and her confused, scanty account finally appeared in 1977. This belated version of that traumatic affair reflects, one suspects, judgments formed over the intervening fifty years. A few scenes are powerfully presented, but the overwhelming air of weariness in the account, and its anti-Semitic and McCarthy-like tone toward the agitators and their leaders is distasteful.

Porter's version of the Sacco and Vanzetti affair as reported by Lopez in *Conversations with Katherine Anne Porter* is more palatable. In this version, "Seven Days in a Boston Jail," she is a charmingly loquacious storyteller, not a jaded and world-weary author.

Mexican Arts and Crafts

Porter's *Outline of Mexican Popular Arts and Crafts* (1922) is one of her most important and little-known essays. It has never been reprinted and is difficult to find, though it contains her most perceptive comments on Mexican art. In the first paragraph she notes: "In this country the past is interwoven visibly with the present, living and potent." As she explored the Mexican past, Givner notes, Porter had "her first exposure to a coherent, consciously articulated aesthetic philosophy, and she was profoundly affected by it. Ever afterward she incorporated her ideas on Mexican art into her own aesthetic theory, expressing frequently in her discussions of her own work, the opinion that the artist must draw his strength from his roots and from his familiar world."[7]

Porter, unknown to the literary world in 1922, seems to have been stating her own developing creed in the *Outline*: "The first concern of the scientist is to discover the origin, the first impulse of the artist is to apprehend the spirit. If the artist has more nearly achieved his aim, it is maybe because his task is simpler. He perceives and accepts the fundamental kinship of all human beings on the plane of natural emotion." It is unfortunate that this important document was not included in Porter's *Collected Essays*.

Porter's essays and occasional writings show her at her best and at her worst. At times she is the high priestess of art and at other times she is a confused writer without a firm grip on her material. Indeed, these writings remain, as she correctly judged them to be, a journal of her "thinking and feeling."

Chapter Seven

Conclusion

My father once said, "If you want to write, you can write just as well here at home. Besides, what business has a lady writing? Why not write letters to your friends."—Katherine Anne Porter.[1]

Katherine Anne Porter considered herself an artist: "I'm one of the few living people not afraid to pronounce that word," she said in 1958. "Even Hemingway and Faulkner don't say they are artists. I've wondered why people interested in the mind and human heart have been intimidated."[2] During her entire career she went her own artistic way, and in her writing she consistently told a "straight story." When she began writing, stories had to be written according to "a slick formula that was being used by the magazines and being practiced with great skill by a handful of craftsmen."[3] Porter "wrote honest," and honest stories then and now have limited popular acceptance. Her critical reputation began to grow with the publication of *Flowering Judas* in 1930, but until *Ship of Fools* appeared in 1962 she was never widely read.

Porter's short stories are marked by a mastery of technique, by honesty, and by a desire to explore the human heart and mind and society itself, without lapsing into popular clichés. Whether she was writing about Mexicans, Texans, the Irish, or Germans, one feels that she knew her people and their backgrounds perfectly. She lived and relived the experiences and emotions of her characters so thoroughly that she was often able to write the final versions of her stories and short novels in a matter of hours or days.

Porter had developed her fictional techniques by the time she published her first story, and technically she showed little improvement afterwards. She was a conscious artist, in the tradition of Cather, James, and Joyce; she knew what she wanted to say and what mood she wished to create. Just how demanding her high standards were is best illustrated by a careful reading of the slim volume of her work. One finds story after story of near perfection. Some stories such as "Flowering Judas," "The Circus," "The Grave," and "Noon Wine" have been widely anthologized and analyzed, but they are not superior to "He" or "The Downward Path to Wisdom."

She dealt with important themes in her fiction; James William Johnson suggests that her themes were "of the individual within his heritage," of "cultural displacement," of unhappy marriages and the accompanying self-delusion, of "the death of love," of "man's slavery to his own nature and subjugation to a human fate which dooms him to suffering and disappointment." One might retitle, reorder, expand or contract these categories, as other critics have done, but Johnson's succinct listing of her themes remains a valid summary of Porter's main fictional concerns.

She explored constantly the chaos of the universe and the forces within people and society that lead to human alienation. Her probings of the human condition were deeply personal and yet, because of the constant play of irony in everything she wrote, impersonal and universal also.

Her often and justly praised style is never mannered, is perfectly adapted to her material, and is marked by clarity. She consciously avoided stylistic characteristics or peculiarities that would make her work trite or easily imitated. No skeleton keys are needed to unlock her stories or her style. She learned from Sterne, Virginia Woolf, Joyce, James, and others, but she did not in her mature style imitate them. She set out to write in her own way, simply and clearly, flowingly and flawlessly. She used her admirable style to create characters of complexity who grip the imagination: María Concepción, Braggioni, Miranda, Stephen, Homer T. Hatch, Papa Müller, to name only a few. She also re-created with authority the social climate of Mexico, of turn-of-the-century Texas, of Denver during wartime, and the slums of New York during the depression of the 1930s.

Her rank as a major short story writer is assured. Her stories should be compared, as Robert Penn Warren rightly asserts, with those of Joyce, Hemingway, Katherine Mansfield, and Sherwood Anderson. Her essays and book reviews, because of the press of time and the circumstances under which they were written, are generally not so carefully fashioned as the stories, though they do add insight into Porter's craftsmanship and the sources of her art.

The long delay before the completion and publication of *Ship of Fools* was gossiped about for years, and the novel's unexpected (to Porter) success—and particularly its Book-of-the-Month-Club sponsorship—led immediately to damnation of its author by some critics. There were innuendoes that Porter had abandoned her high artistic standards in order to gain popular success. All the evidence is against this view, we think. She says she wrote the book she set out to write, and *Ship of Fools* does not pander to middle-class taste or morality. The theme of the novel could hardly give aid and comfort to any class or nationality. The novel is more than a series of vignettes, for it is carefully planned, each sketch integrated into the allegorical, political, social, and psychological themes Porter chose to explore. It is a candid, frank, realistic, symbolic story that brings together Porter's knowledge of the world and its people, and in it she demonstrated that her artistic powers were not diminished. Though most readers will continue to favor her short fiction, this one long work does not detract from her great power as an artist.

Porter lived a long and difficult life. Her family and her particular social background did not encourage her artistic aspirations nor foreshadow her accomplishments. Her personal life was more often chaotic than tranquil, but she persevered and completed a significant body of literary works, stories that seem timeless in their appeal.

Porter was correct in her self-estimation: she was an artist. She was, in fact, an artist of the first rank.

Notes and References

Chapter One

1. "Notes on Writing," *The Collected Essays and Occasional Writings of Katherine Anne Porter* (New York: Delacorte Press, 1970), 449.
2. "Katherine Anne Porter," *Twentieth Century Authors* (New York: H. W. Wilson Co., 1942), 1118–19.
3. Archer Winsten, "Presenting the Portrait of an Artist," *New York Post*, 6 May 1937, 17.
4. Joan Givner, *Katherine Anne Porter: A Life* (New York: Simon & Schuster, 1982), 67. This entire chapter is heavily indebted to Givner's biography.
5. Ibid., 91.
6. Ibid., 92.
7. "Reflections on Willa Cather," *Collected Essays*, 33.
8. Givner, *Katherine Anne Porter*, 131–40.
9. For accounts of the genesis of "Flowering Judas," see ibid., 154–56, 217–19; Thomas F. Walsh "The Making of 'Flowering Judas,' " *Journal of Modern Literature* 12 (March 1985):109–30; and for background information on Porter in Mexico see also Darlene Harbor Unrue, *Truth and Vision in Katherine Anne Porter's Fiction* (Athens: University of Georgia Press, 1985).
10. Givner, *Katherine Anne Porter*, 51. Givner has written convincingly about Porter's father: He was an intelligent, sensitive man but "of no substance, ineffective in his personal relationships. . . . As he grew older . . . his character deteriorated. Always vain and irascible, he became hostile, violent, and uncontrolled" (47–48).
11. Brom Weber, ed., *The Letters of Hart Crane 1916–1932* (New York: Hermitage House, 1952), 378. For detailed accounts of the Porter-Crane episode, see Givner, *Katherine Anne Porter*, 234–37 and John Unterecker, *Voyager: A Life of Hart Crane* (New York: Farrar, Straus & Giroux, 1969), 658–96.
12. See Givner, *Katherine Anne Porter*, 243–68 for an account of Porter's stay in Germany. Givner has information on Porter's anti-Semitism in this section and on 450–51.
13. Elinor Langer, *Josephine Herbst: The Story She Could Never Tell* (Boston: Little, Brown & Co., 1984), 251–56.
14. Givner, 504–6.

Chapter Two

1. Charles A. Allen, "Katherine Anne Porter: Psychology as Art," *Southwest Review* 41 (Summer 1956):225; Jane Krause DeMouy, *Katherine Anne Porter's Women* (Austin: University of Texas Press, 1983), 21–27; Givner, *Katherine Anne Porter,* 160–63; James Hafley, " 'María Concepción': Life among the Ruins," *Four Quarters* 12 (November 1962):11–17; John Edward Hardy, *Katherine Anne Porter* (New York: Frederick Ungar, 1973), 63; James William Johnson, "Another Look at Katherine Anne Porter," *Virginia Quarterly Review* 36 (Autumn 1960):605, 608, 611; M. M. Liberman, *Katherine Anne Porter's Fiction* (Detroit: Wayne State University Press, 1971), 59–69; Enrique Hank Lopez, *Conversations with Katherine Anne Porter* (Boston: Little, Brown & Co., 1981), 69–72; Harry John Mooney, *The Fiction and Criticism of Katherine Anne Porter,* rev. ed. (Pittsburgh: University of Pittsburgh Press, 1962), 47–48; William L. Nance, S. M., *Katherine Anne Porter & the Art of Rejection* (Chapel Hill: University of North Carolina Press, 1964), 12–15; Unrue, *Truth and Vision,* 16–25.

2. Lopez, *Conversations,* 71.

3. Givner, *Katherine Anne Porter,* 145, 162.

4. DeMouy, *Porter's Women,* 27–30; Hardy, *Katherine Anne Porter,* 112–13; Lopez, *Conversations,* 62–64; Unrue, *Truth and Vision,* 106–15.

5. Unrue, *Truth and Vision,* 112.

6. DeMouy, *Porter's Women,* 30–36; Givner, *Katherine Anne Porter,* 171–72; Lopez, *Conversations,* 82–83, 172; Unrue, *Truth and Vision,* 117–20.

7. Johnson, "Another Look," 607.

8. Porter may here be making an allusion to Henry James's *In the Cage.*

9. Lopez, *Conversations,* 82–83.

10. DeMouy, *Porter's Women,* 36.

11. Allen, "Psychology as Art," 227–29; Sam Bluefarb, "Loss of Innocence in 'Flowering Judas,' " *College Language Association Journal* 7 (March 1964):256–62; DeMouy, *Porter's Women,* 78–92; Givner, *Katherine Anne Porter,* 155–56, 217–19; Leon Gottfried, "Death's Other Kingdom: Dantesque and Theological Symbolism in 'Flowering Judas,' " *PMLA* 84 (January 1969):112–24; Beverly Gross, "The Poetic Narrative: A Reading of 'Flowering Judas,' " *Style* 2 (Spring 1968):129–39; Hardy, *Katherine Anne Porter,* 68–76; Johnson, "Another Look," 603–4, 611; Liberman, *Porter's Fiction,* 70–79; Lopez, *Conversations,* 75–76, 142–46; David Madden, "The Charged Image in Katherine Anne Porter's 'Flowering Judas,' " *Studies in Short Fiction* 7 (Spring 1970):277–89; Mooney, *Fiction and Criticism,* 46–47; Nance, *Katherine Anne Porter,* 22–29; "Flowering Judas" in *This Is My Best,* ed. Whit Burnett (New York: Dial Press, 1942), 539–40; Unrue, *Truth and Vision,* 75–82; Walsh, " 'Flowering Judas,' " 109–

30. Robert Penn Warren, "Irony with a Center: Katherine Anne Porter," *Kenyon Review* 4 (Winter 1942):29–42; Ray B. West, Jr., "Theme through Symbol," in *The Art of Modern Fiction* (New York: Rinehart & Co. 1949), 287–92; West, *Katherine Anne Porter* (Minneapolis: University of Minnesota Press, 1963), 9–12.

12. Burnett, *This Is My Best,* 539–40.

13. Walsh, " 'Flowering Judas,' " 109–30.

14. *Recent Southern Fiction: A Panel Discussion, Bulletin of Wesleyan College* 41 (January 1961), 12.

15. DeMouy, *Porter's Women,* 92; Givner, *Katherine Anne Porter,* 155–56; Lopez, *Conversations,* 64–68.

16. Allen, "Katherine Anne Porter," 229–30; DeMouy, *Porter's Women,* 93–111; Givner, *Katherine Anne Porter,* 239–41; Hardy, *Katherine Anne Porter,* 113–15; Johnson, "Another Look," 606; Lopez, *Conversations,* 146–50; Mooney, *Fiction and Criticism,* 38–39; Nance, *Katherine Anne Porter,* 49–54; Unrue, *Truth and Vision,* 26–30.

17. Howard Baker, "Some Notes on New Fiction," in Edward Schwartz, "Katherine Anne Porter: A Critical Bibliography," *Bulletin of the New York Public Library* 57 (May 1953):241.

18. Mooney, *Fiction and Criticism,* 38.

19. Marie Seton, *Sergei M. Eisenstein* (London : Dudley Head, 1952), 195 96.

20. Ibid., 515–16.

21. S. M. Eisenstein, *Que Viva Mexico!* (London: Vision Press 1951), 47–62.

22. DeMouy, *Porter's Women,* 73–78; Givner, *Katherine Anne Porter,* 234–39; Johnson, "Another Look," 604, 611; Lopez, *Conversations,* 201–3; Mooney, *Fiction and Criticism,* 49; Nance, *Katherine Anne Porter,* 37–42; Marjorie Ryan, "*Dubliners* and the Stories of Katherine Anne Porter," *American Literature* 31 (January 1960):470–71; Unrue, *Truth and Vision,* 131–39; West, *Katherine Anne Porter,* 9.

23. James Ruoff and Del Smith, "Katherine Anne Porter on *Ship of Fools,*" *College English* 24 (February 1963):397.

24. For additional information about Porter in Mexico, see Drewey Wayne Gunn, *American and British Writers in Mexico, 1556–1973* (Austin: University of Texas Press, 1974); William L. Nance, "Katherine Anne Porter and Mexico," *Southwest Review* 55 (Spring 1970):143–53; Colin Partridge, " 'My Familiar Country': An Image of Mexico in the Work of Katherine Anne Porter," *Studies in Short Fiction* 7 (Fall 1970):597–614.

Chapter Three

1. DeMouy, *Porter's Women,* 120–22; Johnson, "Another Look," 602; Charles Kaplan, "True Witness: Katherine Anne Porter," *Colorado*

Quarterly 7 (Winter 1959):621; Mooney, *Fiction and Criticism,* 16–18; Nance, *Katherine Anne Porter,* 80–83; Unrue, *Truth and Vision,* 30, 149; West, *Katherine Anne Porter,* 24–25.

2. DeMouy, *Porter's Women,* 127–29; Hardy, *Katherine Anne Porter,* 40; Lopez, *Conversations,* 248–49; Mooney, *Fiction and Criticism,* 16; Nance, *Katherine Anne Porter,* 83–85; Unrue, *Truth and Vision,* 30, 149; West, *Katherine Anne Porter,* 25.

3. DeMouy, *Porter's Women,* 115–20, 122–26; Winfred S. Emmons, *Katherine Anne Porter: The Regional Stories* (Austin, Tex.: Steck-Vaughn Co., 1967), 15; John V. Hagopian, *Insight I* (Frankfurt: Hirschgraben 1962), 212–15; Johnson, "Another Look," 602–10; Kaplan, "True Witness," 321–22; Mooney, *Fiction and Criticism,* 17–19; Nance, *Katherine Anne Porter,* 91–100; Unrue, *Truth and Vision,* 30, 149; West, *Katherine Anne Porter,* 26.

4. DeMouy, *Porter's Women,* 133–36; Emmons, *Katherine Anne Porter,* 15–16; Hardy, *Katherine Anne Porter,* 40–41; Johnson, "Another Look," 602; Kaplan, "True Witness," 324; Lopez, *Conversations,* 248–49; Mooney, *Fiction and Criticism,* 16; Nance, *Katherine Anne Porter,* 100–102; Unrue, *Truth and Vision,* 29–30; West, *Katherine Anne Porter,* 25–26.

5. DeMouy, *Porter's Women,* 136–39; Emmons, *Katherine Anne Porter,* 20–24; Givner, *Katherine Anne Porter,* 196, 212, 434–35, 475; Hardy, *Katherine Anne Porter,* 16–19; Johnson, "Another Look," 605, 609, 611; Lopez, *Conversations,* 30, 203–4; Nance, *Katherine Anne Porter,* 107–14; Unrue, *Truth and Vision,* 45–48, 227–28.

6. Givner, *Katherine Anne Porter,* 170.

7. James William Johnson first noticed Porter's use of Blake.

8. DeMouy, *Porter's Women,* 129–33; Emmons, *Katherine Anne Porter,* 19–20; Givner, *Katherine Anne Porter,* 196; Hardy, *Katherine Anne Porter,* 41; Johnson, "Another Look," 605, 609–10; Kaplan, "True Witness," 323–24; Mooney, *Fiction and Criticism,* 19; Nance, *Katherine Anne Porter,* 86–88; S. H. Poss, "Variations on a Theme in Four Stories of Katherine Anne Porter," *Twentieth Century Literature* 4 (April-July 1958):21–24; Edward G. Schwartz, "The Fictions of Memory," *Southwest Review* 45 (Summer 1960):205–6; Unrue, *Truth and Vision,* 30–33; West, *Katherine Anne Porter,* 27–28.

9. Schwartz in "The Fictions of Memory" points out Huck Finn's similar feelings.

10. Vereen M. Bell, " 'The Grave' Revisited," *Studies in Short Fiction* 3 (Fall 1965):39–45; Cleanth Brooks, "On 'The Grave,' " *Yale Review* 55 (Winter 1966):275–79; Daniel Curley, "Treasure in 'The Grave,' " *Modern Fiction Studies* 9 (Winter 1963–64):377–84; DeMouy, *Porter's Women,* 139–44; Emmons, *Katherine Anne Porter,* 24–25; Givner, *Katherine Anne Porter,* 68–71, 196, 197, 288; Hardy, *Katherine Anne Porter,* 20–24; Sister M. Joselyn, " 'The Grave' as a Lyrical Short Story," *Studies in Short Fiction*

1 (Spring 1964):216–21; Dale Kramer, "Notes on Lyricism and Symbols in 'The Grave,' " *Studies in Short Fiction* 2 (Summer 1965):331–36; Mooney, *Fiction and Criticism*, 19–20; Nance, *Katherine Anne Porter*, 102–7; William Prater, " 'The Grave': Form and Symbol," *Studies in Short Fiction* 6 (Spring 1969):336–38; Constance Rooke and Bruce Wallis, "Myth and Epiphany in Porter's 'The Grave,' " *Studies in Short Fiction* 15 (Summer 1978):269–75; Schwartz, "Fictions of Memory," 214–15; Unrue, *Truth and Vision*, 48–53; West, *Katherine Anne Porter*, 28–29.

11. Charles A. Allen, "The Nouvelles of Katherine Anne Porter," *University of Kansas City Review* 29 (December 1962):88–90; Cleanth Brooks and Robert Penn Warren, *Understanding Fiction* (New York: Appleton-Century-Crofts, 1943), 529–34; DeMouy, *Porter's Women*, 145–57; Emmons, *Katherine Anne Porter*, 5–7; Givner, *Katherine Anne Porter*, 25, 55, 57, 58, 60, 64, 103, 283, 288, 306, 374, 465; Hardy, *Katherine Anne Porter*, 24–33; Liberman, *Porter's Fiction*, 37–51; Mooney, *Fiction and Criticism*, 20–25; Nance, *Katherine Anne Porter*, 114–31; Poss, "Variations," 24–25; Schwartz, "Fictions of Memory," 206–8; Unrue, *Truth and Vision*, 124–31, 237; Warren, "Irony with a Center" *Kenyon Review* 4 (Winter 1942), 29–42; West, *Katherine Anne Porter*, 15–20.

12. Unrue, *Truth and Vision*, 237.

13. Allen, "Nouvelles," 90–92; DeMouy, *Porter's Women*, 157–66; Givner, *Katherine Anne Porter*, 51, 127–29, 299, 305, 306, 337, 351, 410, 433; Hardy, *Katherine Anne Porter*, 76–89; Lopez, *Conversations*, 46–48; Mooney, *Fiction and Criticism*, 25–33; Nance, *Katherine Anne Porter*, 131–55; Poss, "Variations," 23–25; Unrue, *Truth and Vision*, 153–60; Sarah Youngblood, "Structure and Imagery in Katherine Anne Porter's 'Pale Horse, Pale Rider,' " *Modern Fiction Studies* 5 (Winter 1959):344–52.

14. *Denver Post*, 22 March 1956, in Kathryn Adams Sexton, "Katherine Anne Porter's Years in Denver," (Master's thesis, University of Colorado, 1961), 84–85.

15. Givner, *Katherine Anne Porter*, 128.

Chapter Four

1. Brother Paul Francis Deasy, "Reality and Escape," *Four Quarters* 12 (January 1963):28–31; DeMouy, *Porter's Women*, 36–38; Emmons, *Katherine Anne Porter*, 26–28; Givner, *Katherine Anne Porter*, 46–47, 279; Hardy, *Katherine Anne Porter*, 34–38; Johnson, "Another Look," 611; Bruce W. Jorgensen, " 'The Other Side of Silence': Katherine Anne Porter's 'He' as Tragedy," *Modern Fiction Studies* 28 (Autumn 1982):395–404; Liberman, *Porter's Fiction*, 87–91; Debra A. Moddelmog, "Narrative Irony and Hidden Motivations in Katherine Anne Porter's 'He,' " *Modern Fiction Studies* 28 (Autumn 1982):405–13; Mooney, *Fiction and Criticism*, 47; Nance, *Katherine Anne Porter*, 18–21; Unrue, *Truth and Vision*, 33–35.

2. Allen, "Nouvelles," 87–88; Emmons, *Katherine Anne Porter*, 28–34; Givner, *Katherine Anne Porter*, 19, 64, 73–77, 279–80, 299, 306, 314, 374, 409, 465, 510; Hardy, *Katherine Anne Porter*, 97–108; Johnson, "Another Look," 605; Liberman, *Porter's Fiction*, 52–58; Lopez, *Conversations*, 217–20; Mooney, *Fiction and Criticism*, 39–43; Nance, *Katherine Anne Porter*, 55–62; Marvin Pierce, "Point of View: Katherine Anne Porter's *Noon Wine*," *Ohio University Review* 3 (1961):95–113; " 'Noon Wine': The Sources," *Yale Review* 46 (September 1956), also in *Collected Essays*, 467–82; J. Oates Smith, "Porter's *Noon Wine*: A Stifled Tragedy," *Renascence* 17 (Spring 1966):157–62; M. Wynn Thomas, "Strangers in a Strange Land: A Reading of 'Noon Wine,' " *American Literature* 47 (May 1975):230–46; Unrue, *Truth and Vision*, 40–45; Thomas F. Walsh, "The 'Noon Wine' Devils," *Georgia Review* 22 (Spring 1968):90–96; Thomas F. Walsh, "Deep Similarities in 'Noon Wine,' " *Mosaic* 9 (Fall 1975):83–91; Warren, "Irony with a Center," *Kenyon Review* 4 (Winter 1942), 29–42; Glenway Wescott, *Images of Truth* (New York: Harper and Row, 1962), 39–43; Ray B. West, Jr., "Katherine Anne Porter and 'Historic Memory,' " in *Southern Renascence*, ed. Louis D. Rubin, Jr., and Robert D. Jacobs (Baltimore: Johns Hopkins University Press, 1953), 281–82; West, *Katherine Anne Porter*, 12–13.

3. Allen, "Psychology as Art," 225–27; Daniel R. and Madeline T. Barnes, "The Secret Sin of Granny Weatherall," *Renascence* 21 (Spring 1969):162–65; Laurence A. Becker, " 'The Jilting of Granny Weatherall': The Discovery of Pattern," *English Journal* 55 (December 1966):1164–69; DeMouy, *Porter's Women*, 45–54; Givner, *Katherine Anne Porter*, 95, 145, 197, 203, 221, 510, 512; Hagopian, *Insight I*, 208–11; Hardy, *Katherine Anne Porter*, 89–96; Johnson, "Another Look," 605; Mooney, *Fiction and Criticism*, 48–49; Unrue, *Truth and Vision*, 98–101; West, *Katherine Anne Porter*, 9; Joseph Wiesenfarth, "Internal Opposition in Porter's 'Granny Weatherall,' " *Critique* 11 no. 2 (1969):47–55; Peter Wolfe, "The Problems of Granny Weatherall," *College Language Association Journal* 11 (December 1967):142–48.

4. Unrue, *Truth and Vision*, 101.

5. DeMouy, *Porter's Women*, 39–40; Givner, *Katherine Anne Porter*, 197, 198, 205, 217, 221, 352; Hardy, *Katherine Anne Porter*, 41–44; Johnson, "Another Look," 605; Helen L. Leath, "Washing the Dirty Linen in Private: An Analysis of Katherine Anne Porter's 'Magic,' " *Proceedings, Conference of College Teachers of English of Texas* 50 (September 1985):51–58; Lopez, *Conversations*, 210; Mooney, *Fiction and Criticism*, 50–51; Nance, *Katherine Anne Porter*, 15–16; Unrue, *Truth and Vision*, 64–65, 231; West, *Katherine Anne Porter*, 7–8.

6. Givner, *Katherine Anne Porter*, 160–61.

7. Ibid., 197–98.

8. Leath, "Dirty Linen," 51–58.

9. DeMouy, *Porter's Women,* 40–44; Givner, *Katherine Anne Porter,* 174, 221; Hardy, *Katherine Anne Porter,* 46–47, 124; Johnson, "Another Look," 604, 611; Lopez, *Conversations,* 103; Mooney, *Fiction and Criticism,* 47; Nance, *Katherine Anne Porter,* 16–18; Ryan, "*Dubliners* and Stories of Porter," 471; Unrue, *Truth and Vision,* 6, 35, 59, 146, 172, 226.

10. DeMouy, *Porter's Women,* 7; Givner, *Katherine Anne Porter,* 275, 329, 339–40; Hardy, *Katherine Anne Porter,* 15; Lodwick Hartley, "Stephen's Lost World: The Background of Katherine Anne Porter's 'The Downward Path to Wisdom,' " *Studies in Short Fiction* 6 (Fall 1969):574–79; Johnson, "Another Look," 610; Mooney, *Fiction and Criticism,* 50–53; Nance, *Katherine Anne Porter,* 62–65; William L. Nance, "Variations on a Dream: Katherine Anne Porter and Truman Capote," *Southern Humanities Review* 3 (Fall 1969):338–45; Ryan, "*Dubliners* and Stories of Porter," 467–68; Unrue, *Truth and Vision,* 36–39; West, *Katherine Anne Porter,* 29.

11. Givner, *Katherine Anne Porter,* 275.

12. Ibid., 200–207.

13. DeMouy, *Porter's Women,* 55–61; Givner, *Katherine Anne Porter,* 205, 207, 216, 217, 218, 221, 287, 352; Givner, "A Re-reading of Katherine Anne Porter's 'Theft,' " *Studies in Short Fiction* 6 (Summer 1969):463–65; Givner, "Katherine Anne Porter, Eudora Welty, and 'Ethan Brand,' " *International Fiction Review* 1 (1974):32–37; Orlene Murad, "On Joan Givner's Article . . . ," *International Fiction Review* 1 (1974):162–63; Hardy, *Katherine Anne Porter,* 63–68; Mooney, *Fiction and Criticism,* 50; Nance, *Katherine Anne Porter,* 29–37; Leonard Prager, "Getting and Spending: Porter's 'Theft,' " *Perspective* 11 (Winter 1960):230–34; William Bysshe Stein, " 'Theft': Porter's Politics of Modern Love," *Perspective* 11 (1960):223–28; Caron Simpson Stern, "A Flaw in Katherine Anne Porter's 'Theft,' " *College English Association Critic* 39 (May 1977):4–8; Unrue, *Truth and Vision,* 65–70; Joseph Wiesenfarth, "The Structure of Katherine Anne Porter's 'Theft,' " *Cithara* 10 (May 1971):64–71.

14. Givner, *Katherine Anne Porter,* 173.

15. Allen, "Psychology as Art," 224–25; DeMouy, *Porter's Women,* 61–72; Givner, *Katherine Anne Porter,* 145, 173, 278, 287, 374; Hardy, *Katherine Anne Porter,* 47–59; Johnson, "Another Look," 604, 611; Lopez, *Conversations,* 109, 117–18; Mooney, *Fiction and Criticism,* 43–46; Nance, *Katherine Anne Porter,* 46–49; Ryan, "*Dubliners* and Stories of Porter," 468–69; Unrue, *Truth and Vision,* 122–24; Warren, "Irony with a Center," *Kenyon Review* 4 (Winter 1942), 29–42; Joseph Wiesenfarth, "Illusion and Allusion: Reflections in 'The Cracked Looking-Glass,' " *Four Quarters* 12 (November 1962):30–37.

16. DeMouy, *Porter's Women,* 7, 201; Givner, *Katherine Anne Porter,* 303, 339, 374; Hardy, *Katherine Anne Porter,* 46–47; Johnson, "Another Look," 604, 611; Mooney, *Fiction and Criticism,* 49; Nance, *Katherine Anne*

Porter, 65–68; Ryan, *"Dubliners* and Stories of Porter," 465–67; Unrue, *Truth and Vision*, 6, 63, 98, 146; West, *Katherine Anne Porter*, 29–30.

17. Givner, *Katherine Anne Porter*, 303.

18. George Core, " 'Holiday' a Version of Pastoral," in *Katherine Anne Porter: A Critical Symposium*, ed. Lodwick Hartley and George Core (Athens: University of Georgia Press, 1969), 149–58; also appeared in "The Best Residuum of Truth," *Georgia Review* 20 (Fall 1966):278–91; DeMouy, *Porter's Women*, 166–76; Emmons, *Katherine Anne Porter*, 34–36; Givner, *Katherine Anne Porter*, 95, 98, 171, 416, 434, 466, 475; Hagopian, *Insight I*, 216–19; Hardy, *Katherine Anne Porter*, 15; Liberman, *Porter's Fiction*, 80–87; Lopez, *Conversations*, 247, 279–81; Richard Poirier, ed., *Prize Stories 1962: The O. Henry Awards* (New York: Doubleday, 1962), vii–x; Unrue, *Truth and Vision*, 147–49.

19. Givner, *Katherine Anne Porter*, 171, 434.

20. Allen, "Nouvelles," 92–93; DeMouy, *Porter's Women*, 6–7, 177; Givner, *Katherine Anne Porter*, 47, 61, 152, 254, 268, 319–22, 329, 340, 409; Hardy, *Katherine Anne Porter*, 8, 113, 115; Johnson, "Another Look," 603–4, 607, 611; Liberman, *Porter's Fiction*, 95–103; Lopez, *Conversations*, 173–74, 178–79, 242–44; Mooney, *Fiction and Criticism*, 34–38; Nance, *Katherine Anne Porter*, 69–79; Ryan, *"Dubliners* and Stories of Porter," 472–73; Unrue, *Truth and Vision*, 139–45; West, *Katherine Anne Porter*, 30–32; Edmund Wilson, "Katherine Anne Porter," in *Classics and Commercials* (New York: Farrar, Straus & Co. 1950), 220–21; Vernon A. Young, "The Art of Katherine Anne Porter," in *American Thought–1947* (New York: Gresham Press 1947), 234–37.

21. Givner, *Katherine Anne Porter*, 254.

22. Ibid., 319. Kuno Hillendahl was the name of Porter's sister Baby's first husband. Porter also named the Müller's dog "Kuno."

23. Ibid., 320.

24. Porter, "Notes on Writing," *Collected Essays*, 443.

25. Ibid.

26. Ibid.

Chapter Five

1. Quoted in Givner, *Katherine Anne Porter*, 407; *Newsweek* (International Edition), 31 July 1961, 39.

2. For an extended account of Herbst's reactions to *Ship of Fools*, see Langer, *Josephine Herbst*, 311–14.

3. Porter to Caroline Gordon, 28 August 1931, quoted in Givner, *Katherine Anne Porter*, 249–50.

4. Ibid., 250.

5. Weber, ed., *Letters of Crane*, 367.

6. Ibid., 368.

7. Philip Horton, *Hart Crane: The Life of an American Poet* (New York: Viking Press, 1937), 280–81.

8. Hans Zinsser, *As I Remember Him* (Boston: Little, Brown, 1946), 337.

9. Horton, *Hart Crane,* 303–4.

10. Ibid., 284.

11. Ibid., 285. Horton unfortunately does not include footnotes or bibliography, and his sources are not readily identifiable; perhaps much of this section of his book was based on what Porter told him.

12. Ibid., 369.

13. Ibid., 285. Givner in *Katherine Anne Porter* points out that Pressly and Porter gossiped about Crane's life and that Pressly reported incidents concerning Crane to the Guggenheim Foundation's Mexican Selection Committee, causing Crane to be censured. Porter herself took notes "possibly intended for inclusion in her 'Book of Men,' on the various stages of his drunkenness. . . . In view of her own activity, it is ironic that she should have laid the blame for his suicide a year later at the door of his friends." (237). For additional comments on the Porter-Crane relationship, see Unterecker, *Voyager.*

14. Weber, ed. *Letters of Crane,* 377–78.

15. Horton, *Hart Crane,* 286.

16. Ibid., 287.

17. "Notes on Writing," 449.

18. Edwin H. Zeydel, Introduction to *The Ship of Fools,* by Sebastian Brant, trans. Zeydel (New York: Dover Publications 1962), 7.

19. Quoted in Fr. Aurelius Pompen, *The English Versions of "The Ship of Fools"* (London: Longmans, Green & Co. 1925), 1. Pompen's study is of immense help to anyone interested in Brant's satire.

20. Unrue, *Truth and Vision,* 216. See also "The Responsibility of the Novelist and the Critical Reception of *Ship of Fools*" in Liberman, *Porter's Fiction,* 9–36; and Hardy, *Katherine Anne Porter,* 110–40.

Chapter Six

1. *The Days Before* (New York: 1952), vii.

2. For additional information on Porter's critical theories, see Lodwick Hartley, "The Lady and the Temple: The Critical Theories of Katherine Anne Porter," *College English* 14 (April 1953):386–91 and Edward Greenfield Schwartz, "The Way of Dissent: Katherine Anne Porter's Critical Position," *Western Humanities Review* 8 (Spring 1954):119–30.

3. Givner, *Katherine Anne Porter,* 306.

4. Langer, *Josephine Herbst,* 266; Josephine Herbst, "Miss Porter and Miss Stein," *Partisan Review* 15 (May 1948):568–72.

5. Givner, *Katherine Anne Porter,* 184–86.

6. Givner, *Katherine Anne Porter,* 177–78.
7. Ibid., 166.

Chapter Seven

1. Roy Newquist, "An Interview with Katherine Anne Porter," *McCall's,* August 1965, 139.
2. *Texas Observer,* 31 October 1958, 6.
3. Ibid.

Selected Bibliography

PRIMARY SOURCES

A Christmas Story. New York: Seymour Lawrence, 1967.

The Collected Essays and Occasional Writings of Katherine Anne Porter. New York: Delacorte Press, 1970. Replaces *The Days Before* New York: Harcourt, Brace and Co., 1952, and includes many essays and reviews not in that volume.

The Collected Stories of Katherine Anne Porter. New York: Harcourt, Brace & World, 1965. Includes the stories in *Flowering Judas and Other Stories, The Leaning Tower and Other Stories, Pale Horse, Pale Rider: Three Short Novels,* and the previously uncollected stories "The Martyr," "Virgin Violeta," "The Fig Tree," and "Holiday."

Katherine Anne Porter Conversations, ed. Joan Givner. Jackson: University Press of Mississippi, 1987.

Katherine Anne Porter's French Song Book, Paris: Harrison, 1933.

The Never-Ending Wrong. Boston: Little, Brown & Co., 1977.

Outline of Mexican Popular Arts and Crafts. N.p.: S.I.C.yT., 1922.

Ship of Fools. Boston: Atlantic-Little, Brown & Co., 1962.

SECONDARY SOURCES

1. Bibliography

Bixby, George. "Katherine Anne Porter: A Bibliographical Checklist," *American Book Collector* 1, no. 6 (1980):19–33.

Givner, Joan; DeMouy, Jane; and Alvarez, Ruth M. "Katherine Anne Porter." In *American Women Writers: A Critical Reference Guide from Colonial Times to the Present,* edited by Lina Mainiero. New York: Frederick Ungar, 1979.

Kiernan, Robert F. *Katherine Anne Porter and Carson McCullers: A Reference Guide.* Boston: G. K. Hall, 1976. Extremely useful for both primary and secondary sources.

Schwartz, Edward. "Katherine Anne Porter: A Critical Bibliography." With an introduction by Robert Penn Warren. *Bulletin of the New York Public Library* 57 (May 1953):211–47. An admirable guide, through 1952, of Porter's writings and critical articles about her work.

Waldrip, Louise, and Bauer, Shirley Ann. *A Bibliography of the Works of Katherine Anne Porter and A Bibliography of the Criticism of the Works of Katherine Anne Porter.* Metuchen, N.J.: Scarecrow Press, 1969. Useful for all serious students of Porter.

2. Biography
Givner, Joan. *Katherine Anne Porter: A Life.* New York: Simon & Schuster, 1982. An authoritative biography based on the Porter papers at the University of Maryland and on extensive interviews.
Langer, Elinor. *Josephine Herbst: The Story She Could Never Tell.* Boston: Little, Brown & Co., 1984. Contains a comprehensive account of the Porter-Herbst relationship and allegations about Porter's betrayal of Herbst.
Lopez, Enrique Hank. *Conversations with Katherine Anne Porter: Refugee from Indian Creek.* Boston: Little, Brown & Co., 1981. Porter's recollections should be viewed with care. Lopez also included critical materials on Porter's stories; be aware that in many instances his text is remarkably close to Hendrick's *Katherine Anne Porter* (1965).
Sexton, Kathryn Adams. "Katherine Anne Porter's Years in Denver." Master's thesis, University of Colorado, 1961. Includes source material on Porter in Denver, the setting of "Pale Horse, Pale Rider," and a listing of Porter's signed newspaper articles.

3. Interviews
"The Best Years." *Newsweek* (International Edition), 31 July 1961, 39. A prepublication interview, with information about *Ship of Fools.*
Bode, Winston. "Miss Porter on Writers and Writing." *Texas Observer,* 31 October 1958, 6–7. Porter being charming to a young writer turned interviewer. A stunning photograph of Porter in floppy hat.
Dolbier, Maurice. "I've Had a Good Run for My Money." *New York Herald-Tribune Books,* 1 April 1962, 3, 11. Personal history and an account of the writing of *Ship of Fools.*
"First Novel." *Time* (International Edition), 28 July 1961, 65. A prepublication interview. " 'Of the past,' says Author Porter, peering through the wake of two decades: 'I've survived but I certainly haven't flourished. I think Hemingway beat me to it by about twenty paces. Honestly, I am so tired.' "
Girson, Rochelle. "The Author." *Saturday Review,* 31 March 1962, 15. Some incorrect biographical information, including the year of Porter's birth, but with an important statement of Porter's aims in the novel and a comment on the Germans—"they are just as dangerous as they were"—a remark widely disputed in Germany.
Janeway, Elizabeth. "For Katherine Anne Porter, 'Ship of Fools' Was a Lively Twenty-Two Year Voyage." *New York Times Book Review,* 1

April 1962, 4–5. A detailed discussion of the writing of *Ship of Fools*. More family history.

Lopez, Hank. "A Country and Some People I Love." *Harper's*, September 1965, 58 ff. Porter on Mexico, *Ship of Fools*, and other subjects. It is best to remember that Porter was a fictionist and embroidered the truth.

Newquist, Roy. "An Interview with Katherine Anne Porter." *McCall's*, August 1965, 89 ff. Again, Porter gives much misinformation about her past, but her comments on *Ship of Fools* are particularly interesting.

"Recent Southern Fiction: A Panel Discussion. Katherine Anne Porter, Flannery O'Connor, Caroline Gordon, Madison Jones, and Louis D. Rubin, Jr., Moderator." *Bulletin of Wesleyan College* 41 (January 1961). Porter ranges from family history to original sin.

Ruoff, James. "Katherine Anne Porter Comes to Kansas." *Midwest Quarterly* 4 (Summer 1963):305–14. A wide-ranging interview. The *Ship of Fools* section is given in greater detail in the article below.

Ruoff, James, and Smith, Del. "Katherine Anne Porter on *Ship of Fools*." *College English* 24 (February 1963):396–97. A basic statement on the background and meaning of the novel.

Thompson, Barbara. "The Art of Fiction XXIX—Katherine Anne Porter: An Interview." *Paris Review* 29 (Winter-Spring 1963):87–114. The most extensive of Porter's interviews. A manuscript page of *Ship of Fools* is reproduced.

Van Gelder, Robert. "Katherine Anne Porter at Work." *Writers and Writing*. New York: Charles Scribner's Sons, 1946. An important early interview, with information about her life and her method of working.

Winsten, Archer. "Presenting the Portrait of an Artist." *New York Post*, 6 May 1937, 17. An important early interview with much material on family history and her theory and method of writing.

4. Criticism of Stories

Allen, Charles A. "Katherine Anne Porter: Psychology as Art." *Southwest Review* 41 (Summer 1956):223–30. A valuable psychological examination of a few of the short stories; an especially perceptive treatment of "The Downward Path to Wisdom."

———. "The Nouvelles of Katherine Anne Porter," *University of Kansas City Review* 29 (December 1962):87–93. A balanced study of the short novels; attempts to show Porter's strengths and weaknesses as "artist, psychologist, and moralist."

Burnett, Whit. "Why She Selected Flowering Judas." In *This Is My Best*. New York: Dial Press, 1942.

Cowser, Robert G. "Porter's 'The Jilting of Granny Weatherall.' " *Explicator* 21 (December 1962): item 4. There were two jiltings—secular and religious—the latter being more important.

DeMouy, Jane Krause. *Katherine Anne Porter's Women*. Austin: University of Texas Press, 1983. DeMouy's study employs Freudian, mythic, and feminist criticism. Her facts are often incorrect, but we quote several of her interpretations since they represent a recent school of thought concerning Porter.

Eisenstein, S. M. *Que Viva Mexico!* London: Vision Press, 1951. Contains sketchy script for the movie, which has its fictional counterpart in "Hacienda."

Emmons, Winfred S. *Katherine Anne Porter: The Regional Stories*. Austin, Tex.: Steck-Vaughn Company, 1967. A useful introduction to the regional stories.

Hafley, James. " 'María Concepción': Life among the Ruins." *Four Quarters* 12 (November 1962):11–17. A careful reading of this story.

Hagopian, John V. "Katherine Anne Porter: Feeling, Form, and Truth." *Four Quarters* 12 (November 1962):1–10. A spirited reading, by a critic much influenced by Susanne Langer.

Hagopian, John V., and Dolch, Martin. *Insight I*. Frankfurt: Hirchgraben, 1962. Hagopian gives new critical analyses of "The Jilting of Granny Weatherall," "The Old Order," and "Holiday."

Hardy, John Edward. *Katherine Anne Porter*. New York: Frederick Ungar, 1973. This is a gracefully written introduction to Porter's fiction.

Hartley, Lodwick, and Core, George, eds. *Katherine Anne Porter: A Critical Symposium*. Athens: University of Georgia Press, 1969. An important collection of materials on Porter, including essays by Glenway Wescott, Robert Penn Warren, Edward G. Schwartz, James William Johnson, John W. Aldridge, Eudora Welty, Cleanth Brooks, Ray B. West, Jr., Sarah Youngblood, Joseph Wiesenfarth, George Core, M. M. Liberman, Robert Heilman, and Barbara Thompson's *Paris Review* interview.

Hendrick, George. *Katherine Anne Porter*. New York: Twayne, 1965. Porter was critical of this study; for her comments, see Givner's *Katherine Anne Porter: A Life*.

Johnson, James William. "Another Look at Katherine Anne Porter." *Virginia Quarterly Review* 36 (Autumn 1960):598–613. A classification of stories according to themes: "the individual within his heritage," "cultural displacement," unhappy marriages and accompanying self-delusion, "the death of love and the survival of individual integrity," "man's slavery to his own nature and subjugation to a human fate which dooms him to suffering and disappointment"; and the unclassified "Hacienda," which stands alone.

Kaplan, Charles. "True Witness: Katherine Anne Porter." *Colorado Quarterly* 7 (Winter 1959):319–27. A chronological reordering of the Miranda stories; especially pertinent remarks on "The Circus."

Liberman, M. M. *Katherine Anne Porter's Fiction*. Detroit: Wayne State University Press, 1971. Liberman is particularly good on *Ship of Fools*.

Mooney, Harry John, Jr., *The Fiction and Criticism of Katherine Anne Porter*. Pittsburgh: University of Pittsburgh Press, 1957. A revised edition with a chapter on *Ship of Fools* was published in 1962. This first monograph on Porter is particularly good on political implications of her work.

Nance, William L., S.M. *Katherine Anne Porter & the Art of Rejection*. Chapel Hill: University of North Carolina Press, 1964. Nance argues, "At the heart of Katherine Anne Porter's literary achievement lies a principle of rejection." For a criticism of his thesis and method, see Caroline Gordon, "Katherine Anne Porter and the ICM," *Harper's Magazine*, November 1964, 146–48.

Poss, S. H. "Variations on a Theme in Four Stories of Katherine Anne Porter," *Twentieth Century Literature* 4 (April-July 1958):21–29. An investigation of "the What Is Worth Belonging To theme" in "The Circus," "Old Mortality," "Pale Horse, Pale Rider," and "The Grave."

Prager, Leonard. "Getting and Spending: Porter's 'Theft.' " *Perspective* 11 (Winter 1960):230–34. "The story's central irony is that 'Theft' comes principally through unwillingness to spend oneself."

Ryan, Marjorie. "*Dubliners* and the Stories of Katherine Anne Porter." *American Literature* 31 (January 1960):464–73. An introduction to the difficult subject of Porter's indebtedness to Joyce; unfortunately, the study is restricted to *Dubliners*, ignoring the other equally influential works.

Schwartz, Edward Greenfield. "The Fictions of Memory." *Southwest Review* 45 (Summer 1960):204–15. An excellent study of Miranda and the Miranda stories. Especially good on the conflict of the old and new order and the use of memory.

———. "The Way of Dissent: Katherine Anne Porter's Critical Position." *Western Humanities Review* 8 (Spring 1954):119–30. A thorough study.

Seton, Marie. *Sergei M. Eisenstein*. London: Bodley Head, 1952. Background information on "Hacienda."

Sinclair, Upton. *The Autobiography of Upton Sinclair*. New York: Harcourt, Brace & World, 1962. Background information on Eisenstein and the filming of *Que Viva Mexico!*

Stein, William Bysshe. " 'Theft': Porter's Politics of Modern Love." *Perspective* 11 (Winter 1960):223–28. In "Theft," Porter "correlates [the] corruption of the instinct and spirit with the disintegration of traditional religious authority."

Unrue, Darlene Harbour. *Truth and Vision in Katherine Anne Porter's Fiction*. Athens: University of Georgia Press, 1985. This well-researched study is the best full-length interpretation yet written of Porter's fiction.

Walsh, Thomas F. "The Making of 'Flowering Judas.' " *Journal of Modern Literature* 12 (March 1985):109–30. Walsh is engaged in important research on Porter, and this article is one of the best written to date on her work.

Warren, Robert Penn. "Irony with a Center: Katherine Anne Porter." In *Selected Essays.* New York: Random House, 1958. Undoubtedly one of the most influential articles on Porter. Her irony implies "a refusal to accept the formula, the ready-made solution, the hand-me-down morality, the word for the spirit."

West, Ray B., Jr. "Katherine Anne Porter: Symbol and Theme in 'Flowering Judas.' " *Accent* 7 (Spring 1947):182–87. Reprint in *The Art of Modern Fiction.* New York: Rinehart & Co., 1949. The most quoted of all interpretations of the story; West presents a much more simplified interpretation in his University of Minnesota pamphlet on Porter, (see below), 9–11.

————. "Katherine Anne Porter and 'Historic Memory.' " *Hopkins Review* 6 (Fall 1952):16–27. Reprint in *Southern Renascence,* edited by Louis D. Rubin, Jr., and Robert D. Jacobs, 278–89. Baltimore: Johns Hopkins University Press, 1953. A sensitive study, especially good on "Old Mortality," but marred by the assumption that Porter was, by birth, a Roman Catholic.

————. *Katherine Anne Porter.* Minneapolis: University of Minnesota Press, 1963. Utilizes much material from the two articles above; a good introduction to Porter's works. After publication, Porter informed West that the stories of her Catholic girlhood were erroneous, and a correction has been added to more recent copies of the pamphlet.

Wiesenfarth, Joseph. "Illusion and Allusion: Reflections in 'The Cracked Looking-Glass.' " *Four Quarters* 12 (November 1962):30–37. A fresh look at a neglected story, tracing influences of James, Joyce, and Tennyson; and an attempt to determine "the function and meaning of the mirror symbol."

Youngblood, Sarah. "Structure and Imagery in Katherine Anne Porter's 'Pale Horse, Pale Rider.' " *Modern Fiction Studies* 5 (Winter 1959):344–52. Now a standard reading of this story.

5. Criticism of *Ship of Fools* and Background Materials

Auchincloss, Louis. "Bound for Bremerhaven—and Eternity." *New York Herald-Tribune Books,* 1 April 1962, 3, 11. A completely favorable review.

Bedford, Sybille. "Voyage to Everywhere." *Spectator,* 16 November 1962, 763–64. One of the few favorable English reviews.

Bode, Carl. "Katherine Anne Porter, *Ship of Fools.*" *Wisconsin Studies in Contemporary Literature* 3 (Fall 1962):90–92. "*Ship of Fools* is an honest, disheartening book. It is not over-written or over-blown. Quite the reverse: it has been revised downward. Its basic image is old but as the author develops it, it becomes modern and more complex. I do not believe that *Ship of Fools* reaches the heights of Miss Porter's earlier work but I am sure it will find a place, if a small one, in our literary histories."

von Borch, Herbert. " 'Die Deutschen sind allzumal grausam, boese und fanatisch'/Dokument des Hasses: K. A. Porters 'Narrenschiff,' " *Die Welt,* 9 June 1962.

Brant, Sebastian. *The Ship of Fools.* Translated and with introduction and commentary by Edwin H. Zeydel. New York: Dover Publications, 1962. Also reproduces the original woodcuts.

Hartley, Lodwick. "Dark Voyagers: A Study of Katherine Anne Porter's *Ship of Fools.*" *University of Kansas City Review* 30 (Winter 1963):83–94. An excellent article by one of Porter's most perceptive critics.

Hendrick, George. "Hart Crane Aboard the Ship of Fools: Some Speculations." *Twentieth Century Literature* 9 (April 1963):3–9. Appears, in different form, in Chapter 5.

Horton, Philip. *Hart Crane: The Life of an American Poet.* New York: Viking Press, 1957, 283–87. Porter's own account of "Crane's spiritual disorder and anguish." Should be read with Crane's letters to and about Porter.

Kauffmann, Stanley. "Katherine Anne Porter's Crowning Work." *New Republic,* 2 April 1962, 23–25. A careful reading; far less favorable than most of the early reviews. Objects that the novel is a portrait gallery, not the allegory it promised to be, that it lacks profundity, and that the treatment of the Jew "gives too mean and sullen a picture."

Liberman, M. M. "The Responsibilities of the Novelist and the Critical Reception of *Ship of Fools.*" *Criticism* 8 (1966):377–88. Included in Liberman's *Katherine Anne Porter's Fiction.*

Lietzmann, Sabina. "Eine Allegorie von der deutschen Gefahr/Der neue amerikanische Bestseller 'Narrenschiff' von Katherine Anne Porter." *Frankfurter Allgemeine Zeitung,* 16 July 1962, 16. A political reading of the novel.

"The Longest Journey." *Newsweek* (International Edition), 2 April 1962, 58–59. "If there is one central theme it may be said to be the terrifying inability of most of these people to extend any comprehension of mind, magnanimity of feeling, or compassion of heart to those around them."

Moss, Howard. "No Safe Harbor," *New Yorker,* 28 April 1962, 165–73. "Miss Porter is a moralist, but too good a writer to be one except by implication. Dogma in 'Ship of Fools' is attached only to dogmatic characters. There is not an ounce of weighted sentiment in it. Its intelligence lies not in the profundity of its ideas but in the clarity of its viewpoint; we are impressed not by what Miss Porter says but by what she knows."

Muhlen, Norbert. "Deutsche, wie sie im Buche stehen." *Der Monat*, December 1962, 38–45. An unfavorable review in a liberal German journal.

"Das Narrenschiff," *Der Spiegel*, 12 September 1962, 74, 77. Nationalistic criticism in the German version of *Time*.

"On the Good Ship *Vera*." *Times Literary Supplement*, 2 November 1962, 837. Representative of much of the English unfavorable criticism.

Paechter, Heinz. "Miss Porters neue Kleider/Missverstaendnisse um einen amerikanischen Bestseller." *Deutsche Zeitung*, 13–14 October 1962. Especially interesting comments on Porter and nazism.

Pompen, Fr. Aurelius. *The English Versions of "The Ship of Fools."* London: Longmans, Green & Co., 1925. A detailed study of this complex subject.

Schorer, Mark. "We're All on the Passenger List." *New York Times Book Review*, 1 April 1962, 1, 5. Especially good in discussion of her use of Brant.

Solotaroff, Theodore. " 'Ship of Fools' & the Critics." *Commentary*, October 1962, 277–86. A slashing attack.

"Speech after Long Silence," *Time* (International Edition), 6 April 1962, 67. "Novelist Porter's implication is clear, and it is the larger import of her extraordinary screed: all passages of the world's voyage are dismal, and the entente of ignorance and evil is forever in command."

Taubman, Robert. "A First-Class Passenger." *Statesman*, 11 November 1962 (Rowalt clipping book). "The ship of fools is a big, worn, rather empty idea but Katherine Anne Porter doesn't mind playing it up." Completely unfavorable review.

Unterecker, John. *Voyager: A Life of Hart Crane*. New York: Farrar, Straus & Giroux, 1969. A good summary of the Porter-Crane relationship in Mexico.

Weber, Brom, ed. *The Letters of Hart Crane 1916–1932*. New York: Hermitage House, 1952. Letters detailing the destruction of the Crane-Porter friendship provide source material for several scenes in *Ship of Fools*. Porter's account in Horton's biography should be read, too.

Wescott, Glenway. "Katherine Anne Porter." *Book-of-the-Month Club News*, April 1962, 5–7. An expanded version is "Katherine Anne Porter: The Making of a Novel." *Atlantic Monthly*, April 1962, 43–49; another version is "Katherine Anne Porter Personally." In *Images of Truth*, 25–58. New York: Harper & Row, 1962. New "story material" about Porter and high praise for *Ship of Fools*.

Wilson, Angus. "The Middle-Class Passenger." *Observer,* 28 October 1962, 27. Charges the novel is "middlebrow."

Zinnser, Hans. *As I Remember Him.* Boston: Little, Brown, 1940. Contains recollections of Hart Crane.

Index